BE BAD!

REAWAKENING YOUR INNER BADASS

CHALLENGE YOURSELF TO LIVE
BIG, BOLD, AND BAD AGAIN

STEVE STEFANIK

Be Bad!

© 2016 Steve Stefanik

ISBN: 978-1-61170-237-8

FIRST EDITION
Designed by Terry Price Design

Published by:

Robertson Publishing™
Fremont, California USA
www.RobertsonPublishing.com

Printed in the USA and UK on acid-free paper.
To purchase additional copies of this book go to:

amazon.com
barnesandnoble.com

DEDICATION

For my mother, in memoriam

An extraordinary lady and an exceptional
mom who always believed in her son.
She demonstrated to all the values of
deep caring and compassion, and showed us what it was to love
unconditionally.

I love you!

OUR GREATEST FEAR

Our deepest fear is not that we are inadequate.
Our deepest fear is that we are powerful beyond measure.
It is our light, not our darkness, that most frightens us.
We ask ourselves, "Who am I to be
brilliant, gorgeous, talented, and fabulous?"
Actually, who are you not to be?
You are a child of God.
Your playing small doesn't serve the world.
There's nothing enlightened about shrinking so that
other people won't feel insecure around you.
We are all meant to shine, as children do.
We are born to manifest the glory of God that is within us.
It's not just in some of us; it's in everyone.
And as we let our own light shine,
we unconsciously give other people
permission to do the same.
As we are liberated from our own fear,
our presence automatically liberates others.

— *Marianne Williamson* —

ACKNOWLEDGEMENTS

My sincere appreciation goes to the many teachers who led me to see the world differently and step into my unique power. Thank you Tony Robbins, Richard Strozzi-Heckler, Fernando Flores, Toby Hecht, Gabriel Acosta-Mikulasek, and the other countless leaders who shared their wisdom with me through decades of workshops, presentations, books and conversations. When the student is ready, the teacher reveals himself, and I am grateful for all those teachers, coaches and special friends who magically revealed themselves to me as I travelled on my journey.

To the spiritual leaders who guided me to see the light again, I say "thank you."

I am extremely grateful to my lifelong coach and extraordinary friend, Alyson Alexander, who has always seen my gifts and guided me through life's darkest paths.

Thank you to my brother, Scott, for being the sounding board for my musings and shifting moods. His constant presence helped me stay the course.

TABLE OF

CONTENTS

PROLOGUE

———————

TURNING TRAGEDY INTO GROWTH

*"Bad things do happen; how I respond to them defines
my character and the quality of my life. I can choose to sit in
perpetual sadness, immobilized by the gravity of my loss,
or I can choose to rise from the pain and treasure the
most precious gift I have − life itself."*
−Walter Anderson−

As we travel our paths we encounter moments both good and bad that reshape the very core of who we are. Sometimes they are subtle signposts and sometimes they are events beyond our imaginations. In my life I have faced both the subtle signposts and those tragic events beyond what we believe could be true. Yet, I choose to rise above the obstacles and utilize God's gifts to me. I believe He has blessed me with a powerfully unique life of events that has shaped me to be the man I am today.

My path of transformation began in 2008. First, I quit my corporate career where I had lost myself and burned out. I then started my own business to pursue my passion of coaching full-time. Then in 2010, I left my marriage after 22 years and three children. During this time of change, I was dealing with all the complications that a major reset in life encompasses, especially when it crosses multiple domains. I was transitioning through divorce, new family dynamics, career shifts, health issues, being single at 50, and new relationship concerns. Then, in the fall of 2014, I tragically and unexpectedly lost my mom, and my dad passed less than a year later after a year-long battle of strife, grief and pain. Yet in the midst of all this darkness, I began to see some light. I began to see a light that told me that I could overcome all of life's challenges. Not only can I move through life's obstacles, but I have the skills, education, experience, and God-given talents to see the light in others and help them move through their hardest times as well.

THEN, IN THE MIDST OF ALL THIS DARKNESS, I BEGAN TO SEE SOME LIGHT

I began writing this book in March of 2015 as a way to solidify my path in the midst of this turbulent time. As I have grown through my journey, I have realized four key focus areas that were critical and instrumental to my survival during these intense times:

- Mindset
  I had the right mindset: In the hardest of times I believed I could be at my best. I believed I was capable of handling what was unimaginable. I knew I was not only going to survive but that I was also going to thrive and move forward in a powerful way.

- Physical Ability
  I had an unstoppable energy deep within me. I was able to summon this power in an unbelievable way to support me when all seemed hopeless.

- Education
  I had been driven internally for 20 years to seek and learn new insights, stories, and strategies that have given me the tools and ability to manage this transformation.

- Spiritual Practices
  Surrendering to a higher power for the first time in my life, I released the burden of trying to figure it all out. I had faith that regardless of what happened, something profound and powerful was going to come from it.

PROLOGUE

As I have reflected on the past five decades of my life, I noticed that these powers have always been available to me. They have repeatedly surfaced in my past to support me through my most critical transitions. I believe that these critical observations I have made through my life's journey can also apply to others. Through coaching hundreds of people over the past decade, I have realized that these powers are in others, too. Yet like me, these powers have been tucked away deep inside us, only being called to duty at the most desperate times of need. In the darkest times of my life, I have summoned these resources to help me, and I feel the need to help others access their innate powers as well. I feel called to help support others through their own transitions and transformations, and empower them to step into their unique purpose, passion, and power.

When you access these insights from depths that you have not reached to before, you step into the ultimate power of your unique being. You become unstoppable at not only getting through difficult transitions in life, but also empowering you to live the life of your dreams.

> WHEN YOU ACCESS THE INSIGHTS OF THE FOUR FOCUS AREAS—*MINDSET, PHYSICAL ABILITY, EDUCATION, & SPIRITUAL PRACTICES*—YOU STEP INTO THE ULTIMATE POWER OF YOUR UNIQUE BEING.

My book is about bringing this power out from the unconscious, and developing the insights and practices to leverage this power in your everyday life.

I call this "Stepping into your Badass." Becoming Big, Bold, and Bad again. Join me as we walk through how to access all your God-given talents to step up to an extraordinary life.

TIME TO CHANGE

FINDING PURPOSE

The path of your life brightens and changes for good the day you realize that nothing will change unless you do. It is the day you make new decisions. It is the day you just . . . WAKE UP! I awoke to my purpose October 2003 in an abrupt fashion. It was as if the covers were torn off my bed in the wee hours of the morning by a military drill sergeant shouting, "*WAKE UP. GET YOURSELF OUT OF BED, AND CLAIM YOUR LIFE NOW!*"

I was wrapping up a four-week sabbatical from Palm, Inc. that included spending some precious time with my family, a solo fly-fishing adventure through the Eastern Sierra and Yosemite, and finally, a trip to Los Angeles to attend a leadership course.

I arrived in casual business attire for what I thought was a leadership workshop for executives and business professionals—just like every other leadership conference I had attended in the past 20 years. I was excited to be here and get my mind back into the business mode before I began working again. Yet something unexpected was about to happen. As I introduced myself to the other participants, I quickly discovered that I was the only corporate professional among them. To my astonishment, coaches, therapists, and their clients filled the room. The participants I began to meet were trying to overcome some of the darkest, deepest challenges we can face as humans, ranging from drug addiction to sexual abuse. So much for a conservative business group!

I approached the conference leader and questioned whether this was the right type of course for me. He calmly said with a great leadership presence, "Steve, you are free to leave if you so wish, but I believe this could be a life-changing course for you if you stay." I trusted his advice since we had indirectly worked together in the past, and perhaps my "command and control" mind was relaxed after being off work for several weeks. This would just be part of the adventure of my sabbatical, I figured. I stepped back into the room and began my journey along the path of WAKING UP and fully experiencing the life I was meant to lead.

Like most transformational work, the basic process is the releasing of the old and introduction of the new. The releasing of the old is where most people resist, and I was no different.

I began to see that my perceptions of the world were very fixed, to say the least; they were cemented in my body and mind by my experiences, starting the instant I came into this world. These deeply embedded patterns actually extended into the history of my family and played a big role in shaping who I am today. The releasing of the old felt painful, and I questioned whether it was necessary. With the other participants' encouragement, I was able to step into this process of transformation.

UNLEASH THE BIGGEST, BOLDEST, AND BADDEST POWER WITHIN YOU IN EVERYTHING YOU DO.

After spending five days together, I realized they were my peers; I felt compelled to become friends. They faced life's deepest, darkest challenges with a real authentic presence that inspired them to survive and succeed. In addition, most of them took on the task of helping others pass through similar dark times, and that spoke to me as if it were a message from the heavens above.

At that point I realized, "I've found my purpose! This is what I'm called to do—to be a coach, to help others through life transitions."

INTRODUCTION

MY MISSION

My mission for writing this book is to help lead and support people along this same journey: to find their purpose on Earth. I want to empower you to have the courage to step into your own darkness and find the light that not only lifts you to your highest plateau of life but also inspires others around you. Most of all, I want to unleash the Biggest, Boldest, and Baddest power within you in everything you do. Many people have accomplished this, and they are no different from you. The distinction is that they know their specific purpose and passion, and they have staked claim to their unstoppable power. This power is available within every human being, and it is time for you to awaken it. Are you ready to awaken your sleeping giant, your Badass?

Let me ask you a few questions—

- Are you at a point in your life where you feel stuck, or worse, resigned that this is all there is?
- Have you let life shape you and shift you off your life purpose or away from who you truly are?
- Have you forgotten or hidden away the unique and powerful self you are?
- When was the last time you felt truly unstoppable?

Unstoppable is defined as feeling fully alive, confident, as if nothing is going to stop you. You were at the top of your game. You were Big, Bold, and Bad! Is it time to reclaim your true Self, your Badass?

THE JOURNEY

"I am mad as Hell, and I am not going to take this anymore!"

This quote from the 1976 Academy Award-winning movie, Network, is a rallying cry for us to wake up, summon our omnipotent energy as humans, and try to make a difference. Actor Howard Belle plays a newscaster who is asked to leave a network television show due to low ratings. He is supposed to be giving his last "dignified" address to the viewers to say goodbye; however, he feels compelled to take a big stand for what he believes and to let it all out. On air, he took his stand, and said, "I am mad as Hell, and I am not going to take it anymore." He then told viewers at home to get up, go to the window, and yell, "I am mad as Hell, and I am not going to take this anymore!"

This powerful scene called to me deep in my soul at an early age. It has stuck with me for almost four decades and is now resurfacing in the opening of this book. This quote has been a rallying cry for me to make major transitions in my life.

Is it time to take a stand for who you are and what you believe? Is it time to "Be Bad" and rediscover your Badass side? Taking a stand involves believing in yourself, leveraging your unique passion, and following through with your life's purpose. I call this living your three P's: Purpose, Passion, and Power!

Get ready to take a stand for yourself and say, "I am mad as Hell, and I am not going to take this anymore!" Stand up and yell at the top of your lungs, "This is my life, and I deserve to Be Big, Bold, and Bad again. I am a Badass!"

On our journey into the future, sometimes the road is unclear, our travels dangerous, and the route blocked by barriers and limitations. If our internal drive is strong, our intention is set, and our energy is summoned to do what we know is right, we are surely going to arrive at our desired destination.

The poem entitled *The Journey,* by Mary Oliver helps to illustrate this point.

THE JOURNEY

One day you finally knew
what you had to do, and began,
though the voices around you
kept shouting
their bad advice—
though the whole house
began to tremble
and you felt the old tug
at your ankles.
"Mend my life!"
each voice cried.
But you didn't stop.
You knew what you had to do,
though the wind pried
with its stiff fingers
at the very foundations,
though their melancholy
was terrible.
It was already late
enough, and a wild night,
and the road full of fallen
branches and stones.
But little by little,
as you left their voices behind,
the stars began to burn
through the sheets of clouds,
and there was a new voice
which you slowly
recognized as your own,
that kept you company
as you strode deeper and deeper
into the world,
determined to do
the only thing you could do—
determined to save
the only life you could save.

—Mary Oliver—

BE **BAD**!

While my journey to reclaim my Badass began in 2003, what appeared to be a standard leadership course completely shifted my trajectory in life, revealed a new path to travel, and stirred me up in a big way, I would not know to what level until I stood up, frustrated, in 2008 and began to yell, "I am mad as Hell, and I am not going to take this anymore!" That was the year I started to realize who I was and what I was called to do. I woke up only to realize that I had let myself slip away somehow and had hidden a vital part of myself, preventing me from expressing my full potential. I had traveled a path away from my core self, yet now I finally arrived at the pivotal place—the moment to get back on my path and reclaim my core self, my Badass.

The process began with a lot of pain. I felt like I was losing a piece of myself each day when I got into my car to travel 45 minutes to work. I was gradually dying inside, and it took every bit of energy I could muster to survive the workday. Have you ever felt this pain? In 2008 I reached a pain threshold, known to me now as "burnout." This stage left me no choice but to take a stand for myself.

I left my corporate career in January 2009 to launch my own business called INHOUSE COACH. The process of reclaiming my life continued as I began to realize I was in a marriage that no longer served my (now) ex-wife or me. Our marriage of 22 years left us both hurt and unhappy on a daily basis, and I knew it was time to take a stand and get a divorce.

The process of taking a stand is an endless stream of vicissitudes. It is a rediscovery of yourself at the deepest and sometimes darkest edges of your being. It is a reclassification of what is now important in your life and a reinterpretation of everything you think is true and real about your life. For me, every system, process, and common sense I knew, learned or experienced were no longer valid or true. My head was spinning with countless questions as I entered a new phase of my life that I wasn't quite used to yet: What are now the important things in my career? What is important to me in relationships? What is my new role as a dad? Who are my friends now as a single man? What have I accomplished in the past four and a half decades of my life? Who is the new Steve Stefanik? The questions were endless in this space of freedom. However, these stands and reflections allowed me to begin the process of re-centering myself into my life.

As my life continued to unfold, additional health and parenting issues started to surface. The landscape was now filled with challenges that appeared to be insurmountable. Yet the task was at hand as is revealed in the saying, "God and the Universe bring you the biggest challenges when you are ready for them." The process of transformation was intense, but I had the drive to survive and never give up.

Our biology is hardwired to do whatever it takes to survive; therefore, no matter how hard the path became, I continued to move forward. I realized that I could not rush through life's challenges. They seem to resolve themselves at their own pace no matter how hard we push. Instead, the wisdom of time taught me to focus on who I was and then shed the old patterns, processes, and language that were keeping me stuck in the darkness. In their place, I began to allow in new practices, new views, new language, and a new focus to shift my perceptions and adjust my outcome. My life was showing up again. I was beginning anew.

The changes I made were a bit daunting, and some are still not complete, but I am back! Supersonic Steve Stefanik is back in the driver's seat of his life. I have coached many people, and I know there are infinite excuses we all use to keep ourselves stuck. Are you ready to stand up and claim this new path for yourself?

———————

ONE

TIME TO CHANGE

TODAY'S NEW WORLD—BREAKDOWNS AND CHALLENGES

Part of making a change in your life is to become aware of what is happening to you right now. This means turning off the autopilot to take full control and begin the experience of seeing and being yourself again.

The following five points will help provide insights for seeing the extent of the challenges you could face in day-to-day life. As you read about these scenarios, allow yourself to experience them. These insights may be something you are currently in the middle of or something that might be coming. Feeling the challenge this influence may have caused in your life will provoke the fuel and emotions, and this is where you will find the fire deep inside you to reclaim your Badass! These five points are just a few of the powerful undercurrents that may have swept you away from the shore of your Badass life. These undercurrents may have prevented you from making progress in many areas of your life. Use these next five insights to open up to why it is so critical to begin this journey now and build the momentum needed to carry you through to the end.

The question now is: Are you ready to generate this energy to recapture your life and become a Badass again? Answering this question may start with one simple declaration— "I am mad as Hell, and I am not going to take this anymore."

BE **BAD!**

YOUR BODY'S WHISPER

The body's whisper is the way the body communicates with us about our behavior and day-to-day activities. The body continues these whispers so that we can make the right changes, stepping in only when we refuse to listen to it. Are you listening to what your body is telling you? Do you wait for your body to react by breaking down before you listen to it?

> TURN OFF THE AUTOPILOT TO TAKE FULL CONTROL AND BEGIN THE EXPERIENCE OF SEEING AND BEING YOURSELF AGAIN

In my coaching work and my life, I have observed that an old behavior is typically undone by a major breakdown of some sort in our health, relationships, or career. This breakdown in our world or body forces us to stop, and we literally shut down. I tell my clients, "The body is continually providing whispers to you that are subtle warnings about the breakdowns on the horizon. The challenge is that most of our lives are so full of noise—externally and internally—and distractions that these insightful whispers are masked from ever being seen, felt, or heard." As we repeatedly ignore or fail to hear these whispers, the body finally says, "I will initiate a breakdown to begin to eradicate the old pattern or problem." This typically happens when we are busiest and most stressed. When we have overextended ourselves to the edge, a common breakdown is a virus, flu, or physical injury such as pain in the neck, shoulders, wrists, or legs. Sometimes the breakdowns are bigger, including depression, cancer, heart attack, or other major injuries.

If you are questioning the wisdom of the body to take over, reflect on your last health-related breakdown or life disruption. Did the health issue provide a catalyst to get you to slow down in your life or change a pattern? The popular belief that we grew up with was to treat the symptoms without looking for the cause, so this reflection may be eye opening for you. In her bestselling book entitled *Heal Your Body*, Louise Hay claims that every ailment in your body is an indicator of where you are out of balance in your life. For example, a knee injury can indicate that you are fixed or stubborn. The logic is that the knee is one of the most flexible joints in the body, so if you are struggling to be flexible in your life, a knee injury may develop to show how painful it is to be inflexible and lack freedom of movement in the world. Hay recommends changing the mindset associated with being inflexible. She offers affirmations to help rewire your brain to restore the flexibility needed in your life such as, "I move forward without hesitation" and "I am flexible and flowing."

The body is an amazingly powerful tool that helps us to expand our awareness. It is time to start listening to the whispers from your body. It is time to take action to reclaim your life before your body takes over and forces a major breakdown. The wisdom of the body will eventually win; step up before it is too late.

GLOBALIZATION—A FULL COURT PRESS

The 2014-15 Golden State Warriors basketball team is changing the landscape of how to play and win in the NBA. The old strategy of a low post, half-court power game is being replaced by the run-and-gun sharpshooters of the Warriors. The philosophy of one superstar dominating one-on-one versus the philosophy of the powerful unselfish team is shifting the landscape of the entire league. NBA announcer Jalen Rose stated, "This is not a moment, this is a movement." Stephen Curry and the Warriors' quick, team-centered, and aggressive non-stop play overpowers opponents on both the offensive and defensive sides. The overwhelming pressure caused by the innovators is forcing their opponents to change, but most cannot compete. Their team DNA is not designed to adapt that quickly. Retooling to play this new game—from the ownership to coaches to players—can take years or even decades if they are unwilling to throw out the old and bring in the new.

BE **BAD**!

A great book from the '90s entitled *The Innovator's Dilemma,* by Clayton Christensen speaks of how established companies that were and still are successful refuse to invest in new concepts or ideas. Their business models are designed to feed the established power revenue machine and not to invest in unproven future strategies. This model stops innovation from happening inside established successful organizations. Author Clayton M. Christensen says change has to happen outside of the company in order to be adopted within it. This is just like our nature as humans. Check out the expressions, "If it ain't broke, don't fix it" or "Tried and true." And how about this one, "You can't teach an old dog new tricks"? Our language and habits resist the new game of run and gun and prevent it from happening in our lives.

In my corporate life I began to see a breakdown due to the new, fast, and overwhelming dynamics of the global economy. The game was changing from a low post, half-court power game to a run-and-gun, full-court game. The pace and new mindset drove employees to the edge of their capacity. Everyone started looking for ways to solve the problem of how to compete while keeping their head above water. To compound this problem for employees, companies who were feeling pressure to increase shareholder value and expand into the full-court game of the global marketplace, tried to engage employees to do more and more. Yet the game has changed.

I recall a senior human resources director at a very large mobile company saying, "I know there are issues with our employees, yet we don't step in unless the employee asks for help. It is the employee's job to step up, and tell us if they are having issues." Here is the gap; the system is set up to ignore and even negate the problem. The game of life and business is always changing, and no one is going to step in to help you except YOU. These words from the human resources expert are clearly worth considering. You need to take control of your life. Set it up in a winning way based on who you are. Are you open to retooling your game to play in the new run-and-gun world? My claim is that you have to fully step into knowing your fundamentals, eliminate your old patterns, and step up with courage to drive this new way of playing. You have to be in your Badass to win the game.

Curry, 2015 MVP for the NBA, talked about his style of play. He said, "I am confident in every shot, every pass, every dribble, and every action I do on the court." He knows who he is and never deviates from his style of play even if the shots sometimes don't go in. He is a leader in the game and has become the game. He is not mimicking anyone; he is just being himself in this new run-and-gun world. The Warriors from top to bottom are embracing this new world and reaping the benefits. Is it time for you to take control and shift into the new run-and-gun world in your life and business?

THE SEVEN-YEAR ITCH

There is another interesting pattern that affects us in life and at work. This is the seven-year itch!

One of my gifts is to look for patterns, or signposts, that point to life wisdom. If I notice something happens a few times, I tend to watch for the pattern and then determine how I can leverage it in my work or life. The seven-year itch is a well-known pattern in our society, yet people relate it mostly to personal relationships such as marriage. People like to joke about this breakdown in relationships as if it is a funny coincidence. We seem to take for granted the wisdom that surrounds us in our everyday actions, jokes, conversations, and observations. The seven-year itch is a pattern of life that is useful for designing effective actions not only in relationships, but also in your career. This life wisdom, if not observed in your career as well, can cause a major disruption in your life. Please note: in today's world the time horizons are constantly shortening depending on many factors. Observing the pattern as it relates to your life is important.

It may not take seven years to get through these 7 stages. Let me provide a quick overview of how the seven-year itch plays out at work. One fundamental thing to keep in mind is that we are happiest when we are growing. If we remain the same or even go backwards in life, we are not progressing, and if we are not progressing, we begin on the path to being unhappy. Let's see how observing this pattern can help you see that a change is coming or is needed in your career.

> **Year One**

> This is when we start a new job. Our energy, concentration, excitement, creativity, productivity, and commitment are high. It is a new opportunity in which we know how to survive, and we will bring all of our capacity to the table. We are open, engaging, and we desire to succeed.

> **Year Two**

> We begin to get into our stride and embody the practices of success in our new role. Our energy and excitement remains high. The systems, process, and people are aligning in a powerful way around us because of our desire and commitment to become successful.

> **Year Three**

> We have hit our stride. We are now confident in what to do to be successful. Our 100 percent attention is no longer necessary to get the job done, because we understand the nitty-gritty of the job. We have mastered the role and can start to pull back a bit, yet still be successful at a high level. This is when we begin to reset the balance in our life. This is the beginning of the downhill slide.

> **Year Four**

> We begin to settle into a role where we do not have to engage the highest level of energy or creativity. We have the people, processes, and systems figured out so that we can operate on autopilot. We are still active, but we are able to spend more time in other areas of our

life. We lift our head up and really begin to take in the outside world, spotting new opportunities that previously went unnoticed. Here is where the itch becomes real.

Often good management will notice this shift and introduce opportunities to fill this opening such as a new challenge for the employee in a new position. This cannot be a minor shift like adding a new customer, project, or territory in the same space. The new role shifts us out of our current "no brainer" role to one that requires us to focus 100 percent. If this dramatic change does not happen, employees get bored and continue to be open to new ideas and outside influence.

▸ Year Five

In year five, employees begin to see breakdowns in the current company such as issues we overlooked because of our previous 100 percent focus on our role. We may even begin criticizing the system, process, and our colleagues. We look at things that are bugging us in our role and start to explore what is happening at other companies and roles. This is when resentment sets in.

▸ Year Six

Here, employees begin to check out if nothing has changed. We start to dislike the environment, the people, and the role. We feel stuck and resentful, hoping something will change. Here, employees begin to voice their resentment and concerns about the organization to anyone who is ready to listen. We may even become disruptive on projects and in meetings. Year Six is when we become fed up with the job.

▸ Year Seven

This is when burnout or sabotage becomes prevalent. As discussed earlier, the body takes control and causes the system to breakdown to force the change.

The seven-year itch is my interpretation around careers to give us a better understanding of how to design actions that will keep us performing at our best. It does not apply to everyone, but, as with any observation, wisdom comes from seeing if this pattern helps you to be more proactive in your life and career. Most managers do not pay enough attention to their employees, and they may be in the middle of a breakdown as well. Are you at the beginning or the end of the seven-year process? My assumption is that you are toward the end since you picked up this book. It is time to make changes before it is too late. Please note there are always exceptions. The power is to become aware first. Then make an assessment about your current situation. We are responsible for being our Biggest, Boldest, and Baddest self and taking action to change.

I AM STUCK. IT IS HOPELESS!

I believe people stay in a job that makes them unhappy because they have built a lifestyle that requires them to put up with their existing role and place in life. Putting up with where you are in work or a relationship is a losing proposition for everyone. My work with people has revealed that, to be truly happy, we have to move through those places where we feel we have no options. "I am stuck and see no way out" is a common complaint I hear in my line of work. Yet this declaration is a clear signpost acknowledging that a change is needed. Look at your life and see if you have consciously chosen to adopt this limiting mindset. There are two factors that keep us stuck and make us feel hopeless: external commitments and internal commitments.

▸ External Commitment

External stories take hold of you as if they are the truth. These are stories like, "I have made a promise to stay here," "I have financial bills that I cannot pay if I change jobs," and "My family is relying on me." As we will learn, language is a powerful tool that can empower us or trap us. We sometimes blindly accept our external commitments and unfortunately do not question them until it is too late.

▸ Internal Commitment

Strong internal stories you have adopted can constrict you and hold you back. These internal limiting beliefs put you in a box with no doors to escape. Internal commitments often start with "I" statements: "I cannot find anything better," "I will just hold for a while and see what happens," "I do not want to upset other people," and "I do not deserve it."

One day, I was talking with a successful man by most people's standards who was feeling stuck and unhappy. Overcommitted on all fronts of his life, he was feeling quite resentful and even resigned about his situation. He saw no option to get out. He knew he was on the edge, walking the tightrope of life, and swaying uneasily back and forth between crash and burn or toughing it out until things would slow down. We all know in today's world that no slowdown is coming tomorrow unless YOU slow down. You are the one who has to insist—take a stand—for your own well-being. From his stories, I knew he had closed the door to all other options and was relying on the hope that the outside world would change to meet his need to slow down. He was crossing his fingers that some relief would appear.

Yet from my observations, what typically happens is the body will step in and take control, implementing a physical breakdown of some sort to end the poor behavior. Therefore, we need to introduce new practices to overcome being hopeless and stuck. We need to liberate ourselves by setting ourselves free from every chain holding us down in the little dark spaces. According to Viktor Frankl, an Austrian neurologist and psychiatrist as well as a Holocaust survivor, everything can be taken from a man but one thing: the last of human freedoms—to choose one's attitude in any given set of circumstances, to choose one's own way. My claim: We are never stuck. We are just choosing to be stuck. Are you ready to free yourself from your self-imposed chains?

BE **BAD**!

*"I am determined to be cheerful and happy in whatever
situation I may find myself. For I have learned that the
greater part of our misery or unhappiness is determined
not by our circumstance but by our disposition."*
—Martha Washington—

HAPPINESS FACTOR

Are you happy with your life? Or is your life 80 percent unhappy and 20 percent happy? If so, that equation is off, way off! Many people face internal demons that constantly speak negative words to them, and they have allowed themselves to live with these negative declarations. Thoughts like "You don't deserve to be happy," "You can't be happy at everything you do," and "Being unhappy is just part of life" are usually responsible for keeping people in a state in which they feel they deserve something better, but they don't know how to leave their current position. These negative thoughts make people settle for less, thereby living a frustrated and unhappy life.

Being happier is possible, and everyone deserves to be happy. It is doable; you can be a lot happier than you are today in every aspect of your life. There was a great quote I heard at a Christian church: "When you are on God's path, you are happy. When you are not happy, then you are not on God's path." A simple formula derived from this quote is when you are in your calling, or on your purpose, you are happy. When you are not in your calling, or on your purpose, you are not happy. The Martha Washington quote above speaks to our outlook and our disposition about allowing ourselves to be happy. It is a practice to be happy. We can be happy whenever we want. We can look to our mood, behaviors, and stories to help us create happiness in everything we do.

You can create the routines in your life to make you happy. For instance, laughter is a form of happiness. If you watch a laughing baby YouTube video, will you be happy? Will you laugh? The probability is high that you will. We can switch our mood to be happy in a moment. You might need to define happiness for yourself because many people live in other people's versions of happiness. Find what makes you happy and make it happen. With these insights we can choose to be happy and build more happiness into our life. Many great books and lectures about being happy are showing up in the marketplace since it's a big focus for many people in today's world. Do you want to build more happiness into

WE CAN LOOK TO OUR MOOD, BEHAVIORS, AND STORIES TO HELP US CREATE HAPPINESS IN EVERYTHING WE DO

your life? I like this quote from Steve Jobs: "When I was 17, I read a quote that went something like, 'If you live each day as if it were your last, someday you'll most certainly be right.' It made an impression on me, and for the past 33 years, I have looked in the mirror every morning and asked myself, 'If today were the last day of my life, would I want to do what I am about to do today?' And whenever the answer has been 'no' for too many days in a row, I know I need to change something." Happiness is an energy that helps us wake up each day to look in the mirror and be our best. Is it time to reclaim your happiness?

As you were reading these five insights about our changing world, were you able to see a new possibility of how some of these major undercurrents could be affecting your life?

- Is now the time to take control of your life?
- Is it time to listen to your subtle body whispers of wisdom?
- Is it time to retool your game in this new global game?
- Is it time to scratch the seven-year itch?
- Is it time to stop being stuck?
- Is it time to be happier in everything you do?
- Is it time to do something about it?

BE **BAD!**

SET YOUR COURSE FOR THIS JOURNEY

My request at the beginning of this book is to keep an open mind. Rather than setting a specific goal and plotting out exactly how you'll achieve it, a simple intention is all I ask during the exploration of your Big, Bold, and Bad. "It's amazing how much can be learned if your intentions are truly earnest," Chuck Berry said. Step one then is to state a clear intention like: "I am open to exploring my life and will allow my purpose, passion, and power to be revealed." "I am open to new thinking and possibilities to reveal my path." Stating such an intention will help you stay focused on discovery and achieving great transformation. This process of discovery works best if you leave any past influences and limiting beliefs on the sidelines. Finally, as your world shifts and changes, this discovery of who you are and what you are called to do will help ground you back to your true purpose and keep you on track to fulfilling it. Here are some salient points to help you begin the process and set your intention to ensure success at the end of the journey.

‣ **CREATE A POWERFUL STORY OF WHY THIS JOURNEY IS CRITICAL FOR YOU IN YOUR LIFE RIGHT NOW!**

1. The power of WHY is an emotional connection to the project. Without emotion there is little energy to support you when the going gets tough. All changes and transformations take place at the emotional level, not the logical level.

2. Here are some questions to help you build a powerful story of WHY:
   ‣ How would I describe myself?
   ‣ What makes a meaningful life?
   ‣ Why am I here?
   ‣ Do I deserve a better life on this planet?
   ‣ What is standing between my intention and me?
   ‣ Is it too late to change certain things in my life?
   ‣ If I could be a different person, who would I be?
   ‣ What is my biggest dream?

‣ WRITE YOUR INTENTION FOR SUCCESS AND HOLD ON TO IT. EXAMPLES:

1. *"I acknowledge where I stand today is not enough anymore."*
   Awareness and acceptance are the major steps toward changes in life.
2. *"I know there is so much more ahead for me."*
   Have the belief that you are on this planet for a higher purpose and believe that you can achieve anything. Build the courage to overcome hurdles which now seem insurmountable.
3. *" I know I am responsible for changing my life now."*
   Be real with yourself. Quit masking the pain and suffering. Realize that when you do not take a stand for yourself, the consequences grow exponentially.
4. *"I am 100 percent committed to making this change in my life. I will not settle for less or turn back."*
5. *"I trust I am on the right path and will allow the path to unfold gradually."*
   There is a bigger life force guiding your path. Can you trust that whatever happens is what is supposed to happen?
6. *"There is a greater calling or force guiding my journey."*
   We are on this planet to serve a purpose. Nature is not random in its determination of when and where the trees grow. Allow nature's force, the Universe, and God to guide you.

‣ SET A TIMELINE AND COMPLETION DAY FOR THE EXPLORATION PROCESS.

1. A project will take as long as you allow it.
   In other words, if you do not set a limit, the project may never end.
2. A timeframe will help you stay more focused to achieve success without distractions and unnecessary delay.

‣ ENLIST OTHERS TO HELP YOU STAY ACCOUNTABLE.

1. Consent/permission is a critical component of working with someone. It sets up the relationship with appropriate permissions. Have you ever been with someone who, without your consent, tried

to coach you or tell you what to do or how to think? I am sure you have. What type of relationship ensued?

On the other hand, have you worked with someone who you gave permission to support you? What happened in that relationship? The dynamic of the relationship changes immediately when a trusted confidant is involved. This, I believe, empowers them to be their best for you, to be open and candid with their advice. You also may have agreed to accept their guidance or at least be open to it. This is the fundamental piece of any coaching. If you allow an outside interpretation into your inside world, change will happen. By granting someone permission to coach you, you are agreeing that you are on board and willing to go for it!

2. If you do not grant someone the permission, then perhaps you do not trust him or her. Therefore, you may create a poor environment for either party. Without commitment there is no change!

Do I have your permission to coach you throughout this book?

Let the journey begin! You have the intention set and have agreed to be coached, so now is the time to act. This book is designed to help you discover your Big, Bold, and Bad again. There are three main sections: Be Big, Be Bold, and Be Bad. Within each section there are exercises to explore, discover, and capture each of these key areas along this journey to your Badass. I have included a progress map, a blueprint (see the appendix, page) to journal each exercise as you complete them with your insights and progress. The goal is to have an all-inclusive blueprint/map of your own unique representation that you can refer to along the way as you move into your fullest expression of your Badass. Enjoy the journey!

TWO

BE BIG

The year was 2004, and I had left my corporate job to pursue my coaching career. I attended a workshop about innovative thinking around human development, coaching, and leadership as part of my training to be a coach. During the conference I had the opportunity to learn from some great leaders in the field of life transformation. One was Madeleine Homan Blanchard, who spoke about her new book, entitled *Leverage Your Best, Ditch the Rest*. She was a dynamic speaker, challenging audience members to find their best in what they do and to show off this Bigness in how they approach their business and life. Her message struck a chord in my body, a memory of when I was a person who did not hold back or play conservatively; when I played all out; when I was Big.

Her message stirred an energy inside me, which started to percolate through my entire body at an accelerated rate. Meanwhile, two conflicting voices battled each other inside me. One wanted to Be Big again and show up in all my power. The other was fighting to hide, pull back, and not embarrass myself. The second voice was a protection strategy unconsciously designed in my early years out of a deep-seated desire to stay below the radar. I had acquired this pattern as a child in a house with a dominant father.

As this battle raged in my body, Madeleine Homan Blanchard opened up the floor to an exercise. She wanted to know if anyone would like to express themselves in their Bigness. More than 200 people filled the room, and I was sitting near the back. Everybody, as I recall, looked a little confused by the request. They were probably also struggling with their own internal battles of showing up Big or pulling back. She asked again, and her request somehow triggered me into a Big, Bold, and Bad energy that I had archived somewhere deep within me over the past two decades. What showed up was a big expression I reserved for those times, occasionally in nature, where I just wanted to let go. I spontaneously stood up and belted out my Biggest, Boldest, Baddest Tarzan yell ever. Without hesitating, I yelled at the top of my lungs, "Ah-ahahahahahah!" This primal cry was similar to those I loved in the Tarzan movies, signifying "I am the king of the jungle." It completely engulfed the large room, shocking the audience but bringing a sense of aliveness to everyone.

As you can imagine, the room was silent for a moment, then a buzz of excitement filled the room. The interesting thing about showing up with your Biggest expression is that it attracts people. I had only one friend in the room; the rest were complete strangers. I was new to this discourse after recently leaving the corporate world. I was a fly on the wall in the conference, but after the big Tarzan yell, people were attracted to me and to the power, or Bigness, that I shared without shame or hesitation. As I shared in the opening pages, a quote from Marianne Williamson . . .

"And as we let our own light shine,
We unconsciously give other people permission to do the same.
As we are liberated from our own fear,
our presence automatically liberates others."

My observation was that people are looking for others who show up Big, confident, and authentic and wanting to connect with them. Sometimes people need role models so they can model the behavior they desire.

Sometimes they know they are Big and want to surround themselves with others who appreciate and share in being Big in the world. "Like attracts like."

Of course, I am not saying go out and do your version of the Tarzan yell at the next business conference you attend, but a Big move is standing up to ask a question. Showing up Big will prevent you from holding back in life. It is allowing yourself to take action when all the old habits inside you are trying to stop and pull you back. Showing up Big means you are ready to fully express that entire part of you in an absolute manner.

THE INTERESTING THING ABOUT SHOWING UP WITH YOUR BIGGEST EXPRESSION IS THAT IT ATTRACTS PEOPLE

Perhaps the demons are surfacing with their negating voices saying, "You can't," "You are not good enough," "What will people think?" or "Don't embarrass yourself." Because of these voices, your body is closing down, arms are crossing, shoulders are slumping, and breath is short and contracted. This pattern is part of the internal battle that can dominate most people's lives when it comes to stepping up and being Big in any domain of life. You can only win internal battles with a decision to ditch the old and embrace the new. Are you ready to begin to create the NEW YOU, the BIG YOU, who wins the internal battle every time?

We will begin with several simple exercises to rediscover your Bigness. It lies within you already, and I know it has surfaced from time to time in your life. The key is to BECOME AWARE of your biggest pattern. We will find the foundation blocks and assemble them in a way that will support the Badass skyscraper you are going to build. First, let us prepare ourselves to embark on the journey with AWARENESS.

BECOMING AWARE

Awareness is *becoming conscious and present in your body, your action, your language, your environment, and also to others.* It seems so obvious to become aware as we move through the world, yet this practice is one of the toughest to embody. Awareness will offer a tremendous power (power defined as *the capacity to generate effective action*) to those who learn the skill. Although it's complex to pick up, I will discuss several practices that will help you learn this skill. First, **do you know how not being aware has affected your life?** Our bodies are designed to go on autopilot most of the time as they look for patterns in the environment; then the brain jumps into an unconscious 'I GOT THIS' mode, and you react to the situation. We have all experienced the conversation with someone when one word, expression, or moment triggers a reaction that could be positive or negative depending upon how we have conditioned our body in the past. Awareness increases our alertness to potential reactions. The consequences of not being aware can be enormous.

When we begin to build a new awareness practice, we can look at several different areas to make it easier to break down our focus.

- **Our use of words**—The words we use or don't use reveal our world.
- **Our mindset**—Our mindset reflects how we perceive the world.
- **Our bodies**—Our experiences, positive and negative, have aligned our bodies to respond. This alignment to our past opens up or closes down possibility.

AWARENESS BY LOOKING AT OUR WORDS

There is a saying that goes, "Everything you need to know about a person, you can tell by the words they use." Our words communicate what is going on in our thoughts to the outside world. For example, while coaching others, I hear people describe their past with words that shut down their options for the future. They use descriptions like, "I have tried that before, and it did not work out, and I know that I should not do that again," "I could never do that," "I wish I could, but I know I can't," "I am not good enough," "It is just too difficult," and "I am scared." Words help you see others for who they are and what they care about. If we become aware of our word choices, we can use our language to change our life. A friend told me about an injury she had on her shoulder. She first said, "I am trying to get better," and then she stopped and said, "I am healing my wound, and it will be well soon." Both are different ways of viewing the same situation. "Try" is a hopeful word, but "I am healing" is an active, responsible word choice.

To build your own awareness about word choice and usage, consider several areas:

- **Start paying attention** to the words you use every day to describe your life.

- **Record your conversations** and listen to them to see where your language is empowering the future you want and where it is weakening you or shutting you down.

- **Give permission to a friend** or peer to provide you feedback about your language.

- **Hire a coach** to support you in the process.

(SIDE NOTE: Remember there is no right or wrong, good or bad, about your language. There are only more powerful interpretations that get you aligned with your goals, dreams, and life vision.)

AWARENESS BY LOOKING AT OUR MINDSET

In the mid '90s, I was taking a course called Leadership Entrepreneur Innovation and Power (LEIP). Part of the structure of the course was to bring in outside business "rock stars" to share their wisdom. A blind man with damaged hands appeared on stage. He was not the typical "rock star" I expected to see, but the wisdom from this blind man was clear, revealing, and powerful. He was blind, but he had perfect vision. His name was Russell Redenbaugh. He shared a button with the audience that said, "Mood is everything; narratives are the rest." At the time, I could not understand exactly what it meant, but today, I believe it to be a fundamental insight about living a good life. My understanding today is our mindsets that have taken shape in our life dictate the stories that we can create. Moods/mindsets are everything, and narratives are the stories we then generate to support the perceptions our mindsets produce.

Awareness of your mindsets begins with understanding that you are not fixed in your thinking. Yes, there are places in life where we think that it is just the way it is, but that is never the case. Life is never fixed; it is always changing. Are you resisting the change? It is now time to release that "weak" mindset about life, work, or a relationship, and to find a new mood/mindset that empowers you and enriches your life. According to J.D. Salinger, "If you are not in the right mood, you can't do that stuff right."

AWARENESS BY LOOKING AT OUR BODIES

We have all seen the studies about the power of body language. Fifty-five to seventy-five percent of communication is shared unconsciously through body language. So are you aware of the message you are sending to others? This is a tricky area. Becoming aware of how we show up when we move through the world is difficult. Each of our bodies is uniquely conditioned from our life experiences, so there is no tried and true way to predict how we will show up. The opening I want to encourage is to begin to pay attention to the body: your breath, your shoulders, and your head when you are in conversations, reading this book, or at work. Be an observer of what happens to

WORDS HELP YOU SEE OTHERS FOR WHO THEY ARE AND WHAT THEY CARE ABOUT.

your body when in action. The ultimate goal is not to stop our bodies from reacting to the world; we will always be triggered into some type of reaction. The key is to recover the center in your body in order to ensure you choose how you are communicating versus speaking without being aware of your body. I will introduce a leadership presence practice later to help you recover your body to perform in an optimum mode.

LET US BEGIN TO DISCOVER YOUR BIGNESS

A beginning is such a wonderful place. Like in nature, we humans also have seasons in our life. Better said, we can use the natural flow of the seasons to create some powerful new interpretations that can help us design a Big, Bold, and Bad life. When it is spring, a new beginning, that means you are coming out of winter—a time where you were pulling back your energy to hibernate, conserve, and survive. Spring is a special time with all the new growth, warmth, and amazing energy to renew life again. Spring energy is alive, creative, open, expansive, and new! This is the type of focus I would like you to have as we explore your Bigness that may have been in hibernation for far too long.

I truly believe **we all have amazing and unique gifts that are like hidden treasures of gold**. Like in mining for gold, sometimes our gifts are hidden just beneath the surface or sometimes they may be deeply buried. The key is to know how to prospect for your gold. We all have gold nuggets within us, but many people are unaware of their presence. Of those who are aware, many do not know how to prospect for them and use them as precious assets in their lives.

This section of Be Big will introduce insights and tools to help you discover and find your gold at three levels:

1. **On the surface**—Readily accessible if you know where to look.
2. **Just under the surface**—Some simple tools will be required to excavate your treasures.
3. **Deep level mining**—Here the exploration is more challenging, but the rewards are rich.

JUMPING IN

Over the years, I have found that there are numerous tools available for you to assess who you are. Everything from personality type assessments, DISC reports, customized psychological exams, and even astrological readings. I have done all of them, and some I have done multiple times. The key is to look for patterns to support your true self. These insights provide a unique configuration of how you are set up to perceive the world. One of the biggest competitive advantages in today's world is to be flexible and flow with the changes happening every moment. Knowing "who you are" can help you become your Biggest in the midst of the non-stop bombardment of information and demands on your life.

Furthermore, I have found plenty of amazing tips and techniques available for people at every level of life. These generic, high-level tips and techniques are proven to produce results if you follow the steps, but a big assumption goes along with them. The assumption is that you are clear on who you are, and all the foundational pieces that go along with that are in place. Most people try these tips by using the teacher's approach but frequently this does not match yours. Eventually we fail or, worse yet, burn out because the work they were doing was incongruent with who we are.

You are about to embark on discovering your gold. This is your chance to explore your past and dig deep into how it has shaped you. I want to find out who you are, so that as you develop into your Badass, you will be clear, consistent, and coherent! You might be mumbling right now, you might be deciding that you are not going to answer my questions, or you just want me to provide you with the correct answers so you can get on with it. The power of this work, however, lies in the self-discovery. This is about finding your unique Badass, and with the conscious effort it takes, the answers you are looking for will be discovered and revealed deep inside you.

KNOWING "WHO YOU ARE" CAN HELP YOU BECOME YOUR BIGGEST…

A teacher once used a metaphor about finding our uniqueness. He was clear that everyone is different. There are some similarities, of course, but every person has a unique purpose. He told us to think about dogs. "They are just dogs, right?" he said. No. Each dog is part of a unique breed with a unique purpose. Each breed was created to do one thing really well. Terriers are bred to hunt underground, Labs to swim, German shepherds to provide safety, and sheepdogs to herd. We, as humans, are also here for a purpose. Knowing our purpose is a significant step in self-discovery, which is a vital ingredient to stepping into your Badass. Let us first begin to explore purpose.

OUR PURPOSE

Purpose is the reason why something is done or created or for which something exists. There are three different levels of purpose for each of us. Assessing these three levels will help build a deeper understanding of your purpose on this planet. When we are on purpose, we tend to have more staying power and courage when the road gets bumpy in our projects, career, and relationships. In reclaiming your Big, Bold, and Bad self, the road travelled will have its fair share of bumps, and you will become scared, tired, and frustrated if you are ill-prepared. Here are some insights to help you know the importance of purpose and solidify it.

▸ Purpose 1: *Your personal purpose*

This is the understanding of who I am and how I can contribute to the biggest and best of my abilities. I understand my abilities, skills, talents, and experiences, and use them to guide me to where my passion is fully turned on and my gifts are fully expressed.

▸ Purpose 2: *A purpose greater than yourself*

It is like connecting to a company's vision. Apple, Inc. launched its large "Think different" ad campaign in 1997. I suspect most people aligned with Apple because they wanted to go against the norm, buck the system...be different. This type of purpose is larger than us. It's one where we feel compelled to support and connect to things that exist outside of us. Examples are movements that call to us, such as joining the Peace Corps, Save the Whales, or any other environmental or political cause.

▸ Purpose 3: *My greater "God-given" purpose*
Here we transcend our earthly constraints. We allow the mystical and magical side of life to reveal our purpose. We have faith that we are on God's path, and we allow whatever happens to happen.

These three purposes intersect in a powerful way. Accepting all three will empower you to be your ultimate Badass. We will go into purpose development in the third section, "Be Bad."

Now let me introduce you to some simple tools for **mining the surface level** and discovering the gold that is right in front of you.

BE BIG: WHAT IS YOUR MOOD?

Awareness of our moods begins by looking at how moods are an instrumental part of our life. Here are a few things to consider.

- ▸ You are always in a mood. Do a mood check. What is your mood right now?
- ▸ Moods are not fixed. They have a tremendous power over us, yet we can shift our moods in a moment's notice.
- ▸ Awareness of your moods and the moods of others can bring about incredible changes in your life.
- ▸ Which moods support you best? Do you know how to describe moods in more ways besides good or bad?
- ▸ How do you shift your moods? We do this all the time, yet are you aware of the impact this can have on your life?

Yes, there are places in life where we think, "That is just the way it is," but this is never truly the case, is it? The issue most of us run into is that we are resisting the change. You can always view your situation as an opportunity, a new possibility, or even a great fortune. Yet our different moods can open and close these perspectives. **Numerous practices exist to adjust our moods to make them more powerful for us, no matter how dire the situation.**

Success coach Tony Robbins has an excellent "mood adjustment" practice that he introduced at his "Unleash the Power Within" conferences. As attendees stood up and discussed their challenging life situations, and most of them were very challenging, Robbins changed their mood in a very powerful way. He shared a narrative that says when the attendees announce they are confused or at wits' end, it actually means they are on the cusp of a major breakthrough. He declared, "Victory is near!" To shift the emotional grip the old mood had on each attendee, he asked the 6,000-person audience to stand and, with wild abandon, celebrate as loudly and exuberantly as they could. Imagine 6,000 raging fans cheering you on to step up your game because they believe you are close to releasing the old restriction. Have you designed powerful practices to shift your moods at work, with your family, in your relationships?

Mood is a foundation piece in the effort to discover your gold. We have to practice on a daily basis to maintain powerful moods and to avoid old disruptive or limiting moods. I want to define mood in this way for our work together: **Mood is a long-term, ungrounded assessment about the way the future is going to turn out.** This helps us to see that moods are an assessment, meaning an opinion that is not a fact. Once we set our opinion, moods trigger our brain to find the

"MOOD IS EVERYTHING, AND NARRATIVES ARE THE REST."

Russell Redenbaugh

supporting stories to "prove" that our opinion is right. We have to guard against the power of moods to affect how we see the world, our communities, our careers, our family, and our life. **If we are not aware of our moods and their powerful influence over us, we could become stuck.** In addition, moods are domain-specific, and they shift as we move from domain to domain. They can also stick with us across domains. Sometimes our mood about work is resentful, and when we get home to our spouse, our mood does not shift, so we react and do everything with the mood we brought home from work. We have to be aware of our moods and design a life that uses moods as a tool to become Big, Bold, and Bad again. Remember Russell Redenbaugh's wisdom: "Mood is everything, and narratives are the rest." Here are some insights to help you take the first step toward mastering using your mood to Be Big.

EXERCISE: WHAT IS YOUR MOOD?

1. Build a deeper understanding of moods.

   Moods are not just good and bad, which is how most people describe them. Moods have so much more depth to them. One of the best ways to build awareness about moods in our lives is to break down the generic descriptions and build new distinctions that provide us with a better view. For example, some good moods you may focus on are being grateful, cooperative, dignified. Some bad moods you may want to eliminate are being resentful, resigned, close-minded. These are just a few. Create a list you can reference of both good and bad moods. The better we understand each unique mood, the easier it is to create practices to identify and shift to an appropriate mood.

You can also:

▸ Journal your moods. Spend a week tracking your moods to help identify them. Make notes on your personal blueprint diagram (see appendix, page)

▸ Explore which moods dominate your outlook around career, family, and life in general.

▸ Ask yourself whether certain events or people trigger good or bad moods.

2. **Practice different moods.**

We can identify the patterns for these moods. Awareness allows us to make choices. From choices, we can take actions to create a new mood that better suits our desired outcome.

▸ What do you have to do to manifest the mood of open-mindedness, curiosity, or happiness, just to name a few?

▸ What do you have to do to manifest the mood of resignation, skepticism, or argumentativeness?

▸ What do you focus on? What stories are you telling yourself in each of these moods?

3. **Additional resources to help you shift your moods.**

I have identified four processes to help you shift your moods. Most people know them already but are not consciously using them.

1. **Self-talk**—Once you recognize your mood, you can actually use your own internal conversation to shift to a more powerful mood. For instance, you wake up and tell yourself, "Ugh, another day of work!" Then you realize that's a poor way to start the day, so you tell yourself a different story like, "Today is the first day of the rest of my life, and I am going to have a great day at work." Mood shifted.

2. **External influence required**—If self-talk does not change the mood, there has to be some external influence. This typically requires getting the body involved to break the pattern that has fixed you into the mood. There are multiple options, and it's important to find the ones that will work for you. For example, take several deep breaths to change your physiology, listen to music that makes you move, go for a walk, stand up and talk with others, buy a cup of coffee, eat good food, etc.

3. **Peer group support**—Enlist people who know and care about you. This is like an accountability group of sorts. Sometimes we are unable to shift our own mood, but one conversation with a trusted friend will get us right back on track with a productive mood.

4. **Professional support**—Sometimes life hits us in a way that spins us out of control and into moods that need a professional to support us. Therapists, coaches, and psychiatrists are people we hire to help us recover from these overpowering moods.

APPLICATION: WHAT IS YOUR MOOD?

Now that you have a better understanding and awareness of moods, you can begin applying your knowledge about your moods to being Big. Here are some important steps for you to take:

1. Determine what moods make you feel and act your Biggest and most powerful self.

2. Become an observer of your moods and the power they have over your day-to-day actions.

3. Build a support practice to ensure you have the necessary tools around you to shift your moods.

4. Begin to observe how your moods not only affect you but everyone around you.

5. Bonus: Once you begin to understand and leverage the power of moods in your life, practice assessing the moods of other people to see if they are effective for aligning with you. Can you shift their mood to a more productive one?

BE BIG: DOER, WATCHER, ANALYZER

Are you a doer, watcher, or analyzer? There is a great book called *First, Break All the Rules* by Curt Coffman and Marcus Buckingham. The authors conducted a study on people's behavior related to how they take action and identified three different models—the doer, watcher, and analyzer. How will this help you to Be Big? Part of being Big is understanding how you are designed to work. Being Big requires that you understand your spontaneous reaction to new tasks and questions. Most people rely on one of these three behavior models, so the question is, "Which one is your GO-TO?"

EXERCISE: DOER, WATCHER, ANALYZER

Determine wheter you are a doer, watcher or analyzer. A simple way to determine this is to look at how you made a recent big purchase decision. Say you were going to buy a car. Here is how each person would approach the situation.

1. **Doer**—The first instinct for a doer is to go straight into the heat of the transaction. They will immediately go to the dealer or online to talk with the sellers of cars.

Taking action is their automatic first step, and in the midst of the transaction, they are learning, assessing, and determining the best option.

2. Watcher—Their first instinct is to watch others to learn. This is the classic master and apprentice model. The apprentice does not make a decision until they have mastered the action outside of the heat of the situation, but they are actually mimicking the behavior until it becomes second nature, and then they will take action.

3. Analyzer—Their first instinct is to learn anything and everything they can about the situation. Research is the first step. Once all of their questions are resolved, they are ready to act. These people like to perform the task in their mind to determine everything that will be needed as well as the possible end result before they take action.

I discovered that most clients say they do all three, and we all do, but there is one we will default to when the pressure is the highest. Which one are you? I know I am a doer because I approach life by jumping right in and getting to work. I dance with the people, environment, and situation until I get it right. Take this book, for example. The process I followed was to do a basic outline and then begin. While I wrote the book, the stories revealed themselves, and the stream of thought continued to flow. If I were a watcher, I would need to find a master to learn from. I would consult with others and watch how they are doing it until I felt I have understood the game. If I were an analyzer, I would buy the how-to books, research thoroughly online, and investigate the process before writing the first word.

APPLICATION—DOER, WATCHER, ANALYZER

1. Once you determine your type, you will be able to see how best to create an environment around you to be your Biggest.

2. You can now see how others around you may be set up differently to learn. It is important to take responsibility for your style to ensure your learning is appropriate for you.

3. A doer wrote this book, and most of my directions will be as if you were a doer. Therefore, reshape the content to fit your model to ensure you get maximum impact.
   a. If you are a doer, jump right in and do each exercise.
   b. If you are a watcher, find a doer or a book group to read the book together.
   c. If you are an analyzer, read the book thoroughly once and take notes. Then research the areas that need a bit more analyzing from your point of view. Take the action once you have crossed all the "t's" and dotted all the "i's."

Find a way to incorporate this new observation about yourself into your day-to-day actions to bring more meaning to everything you do.

BE BIG: HOW, WHO, WHY, WHAT

There is a powerful tool I used early on in my coaching career called Spherical Dynamics. It was a detailed assessment tool focused on revealing how your brain is hard-wired to look at problems. The tool is no longer available in the market, yet there is one area I would like to share as part of this Be Big section. This insight will provide another foundational block to help you design for your Bigness.

EXERCISE: HOW, WHO, WHY, WHAT

Imagine an invitation to a party. A friend is inviting you, but you do not know anything about the party. What would be your first question to clarify if you want to go? The words you use will reveal how your brain is predisposed to assess the situation. Not everyone is the same, and no one is better than any other, but the words How, Who, Why, and What are critical to look at how you are hard-wired to see a situation. Some people are confident and comfortable in all four, and others are predisposed to focus on just one, but one of them is always dominant.

Based on the four personality type classifications below, determine your personality type, and make notes on your blueprint diagram (appendix, page)

1. **The "HOW" person**—This person's questions will focus on the future. After being asked to attend the party, he/she will start asking HOW questions: "How can I make this work?" "How will this affect the relationship with my friend?" and "How much fun will I have?" HOW questions can be overwhelming because they are dealing with speculations about the future. However, a HOW person can also envision the future and open up exciting stories about how it will all turn out. All projects should have a HOW person on the team to open up these HOW questions for everyone.

2. **The "WHO" person**—This person's questions will focus on the people. He/she is concerned with knowing everything about the people associated with the

request or project. They will use WHO questions to learn more about the party. For example, they will ask, "Who will be there?" "Who else knows about it?" "Who organized it?" and "Who else have you invited?"

3. The "WHY" person—This person's questions will focus on the details. He/she uses WHY questions to learn more about the specifics of the party. For example, they will ask, "Why are they having the party?" "Why should I attend?" and "Why are they inviting me?" These people are the critical eye we need in our life to ensure we have done every necessary thing before we go forward.

4. The "WHAT" person—This person's questions will focus on the action. He/she wants to act immediately. They use WHAT questions to find out how to proceed. For example, they will ask, "What can I do to help?" "What is the party all about?" and "What do I need to do to attend?" Without a WHAT person, a project is not always done with the right efficiency and effectiveness.

APPLICATION: HOW, WHO, WHY, WHAT

1. How are you predisposed to look at the world? Start to pay attention to the word that work best for you. I have a dominant energy focused on the WHO. It is what has drawn me to the coaching career, and I designed my business to take advantage of this trait. On the opposite end of the energy, I am not a WHY person. I tend to stay away from this area, and I have learned to surround myself with people who can handle the WHY with energy and excitement. You can do the same.

2. HOW people strategize around the future, WHO people motivate people to align, WHY people analyze every detail of the situation, and WHAT people activate immediately. Let us pinpoint your automatic go-to.

   a Which area do you feel most happy engaging in?

   b. Which one(s) drain your energy?

   c. Which one(s) are neutral—no energy drained and no energy gained?

BE BIG: LEADER VS. FULFILLER

In coaching professionals, I realized there is a general rule that stands out like a sore thumb. People follow two distinct roles that vary depending on the action in which they are involved. The key takeaway is that there are places where you are a leader and places where you are a fulfiller. Both are powerful in today's world despite the perception that being a leader carries more power. A person whose nature is to be a fulfiller will have a tough time being his Biggest as a leader all the time.

 EXERCISE: LEADER VS. FULFILLER

What are your natural inclinations? Is it to be a leader or a fulfiller? In the business world only a handful of people are true leaders, and the rest of the employees are fulfillers. A key aspect of leadership is to articulate the future and then inspire others to go after it. Fulfillers are excited and energized to fulfill the company's or client's direction.

So, who are you? Use these questions to find out if you are a leader or a fulfiller:

1. Do you like to specify the future and inspire others to follow?

2. Do you like to fulfill the projects which create the future that the leader specified?

I have found that when people recognize this piece, they can design roles and relationships to feel more aligned and powerful, and in turn, they become more confident. Revealing your foundation and gaining an understanding about who you are add to your ability to Be Big, Bold, and Bad again.

 APPLICATION: LEADER VS. FULFILLER

1. Identify where you perform best and move your efforts toward placing yourself in situations that allow you to strengthen this area.

2. Construct this awareness into your day-to-day actions to bring more meaning to everything you do.

Let us go mining a bit deeper now. The unique treasures that are just under the surface require some minor tools to bring them to light. Here are a couple of tools to help you find these additional foundational pieces of your Big self.

BE BIG: WHY DO YOU DO WHAT YOU DO?

In discovering your Bigness, it is important to determine your driving force. This driving force will help you build the motivation to stay on track. Most of us have not reflected on the question, "Why do you do what you do?" I have worked this tool with many clients over the years, and, believe me, everyone's reasons are different. This is why it is so important for you to find your driving force(s) to help build the Bigness back into your life.

EXERCISE: WHY DO YOU DO WHAT YOU DO?

The exercise for this tool is quite simple to complete, but it will require the assistance of one or possibly two people for a few minutes.

1. One person sits in front of you and for 60 seconds continually asks you the question, *"Why do you do what you do?"*

2. Your role is to respond to the question each time in one or two words. A third person records your answers, or you could use a voice recorder to capture the words you used.

Key points in the execution of the exercise:

▸ The person asking the question needs to be direct. They should not be afraid to push you for the answer, sometimes asking two or three times until you spit out a reply. The pressure to answer the question repeatedly will produce the desired outcome.

▸ No result is right or wrong, good or bad. I want you to spit out whatever crosses your mind without wasting any time thinking. This is a pressure-reaction assessment tool to help open you up to a deeper, more meaningful response.

▸ Say whatever crosses your mind, without filters or alarms in your head cautioning or preventing you from saying it. Why you do what you do is unique to you, and this is a chance to find that motivation to add as another block in the foundation. So go for it!

Once you have completed the exercise, the next step is to look at the list of words you used to describe why you do what you do. Pay attention to several patterns:

1. Take note if you repeated words or said the same thing using different words.
2. The first words on the list are not always what truly drive us. They are influenced by our family, peer group, culture, and community.
3. The remaining two-thirds of the list reveal a deeper level of answers. Once the obvious answers leave your mouth during the repeated questioning, a deeper answer will reveal itself. It is important to pay attention to these answers.
4. The remaining part of the list will begin to solidify your key points.
5. What are the key three words that best describe why you do what you do?
6. Do these words truly represent what is important to you?

 APPLICATION: WHY DO YOU DO WHAT YOU DO?

1. In your current roles and relationships, determine if your three key driving force words are leading you toward success or have you lost your way. If your driving force isn't leading you to success, re-evaluate your path.

2. Look at these key words and see if they inspire you to show up in your Bigness. If not, choose new words to motivate you to be your biggest.

3. Design your key words into your day-to-day actions to bring more meaning to everything you do.

BE BIG: YOUR LIFE-DEFINING WORDS!

I first did this exercise at a Tony Robbins event and was amazed at how I was able to gain clarity into the characteristics that are unique to me and my ability to show up Big. This exercise helps identify key moments in your past that reveal the secret of what actions/characteristics bring you joy and happiness. Incorporate these characteristics into the design of your Big, Bold, and Badass life ahead.

EXERCISE: YOUR LIFE DEFINING WORDS

1. Find a quiet place and time (15 to 30 minutes) to spend by yourself. Look for a place with no distractions.

2. Bring yourself into a meditative state. Once you feel you are in the moment and open to reflections, prepare to go back to some of your unique moments in time.

3. You are going to go back to five specific moments in time, remembering one positive experience from each. Jot down a one-sentence descriptor of the situation, and then move on to the moment in time.

   a. Go back to when you were 8 years old. Allow yourself to remember one positive experience. Whatever shows up first is all I am asking. Experience that moment fully, and then write the moment you remembered in your journal.

   b. Repeat this exercise for ages 12, 16, 20, and 24.

Once you have completed the exercise, go back to review the moments you remembered and look to discover the impact they had on your life.

What word best describes your characteristics or attributes because of those events?

To help you more fully understand the exercise, here are the results I discovered:

My words to describe my five unique traits are adventurer, treasure seeker, big energy, learner, and leader. As an 8-year-old boy in the '60s when the United States was on a quest to reach the moon, astronauts were my heroes. I wrote to the astronauts and received a letter back from them. This was the memory that I recalled during the exercise. I realized these travelers to faraway places were true adventurers, and this connected to who I was or wanted to be. I discovered that if adventure is missing in my life, I am not playing at my Biggest. As I dissected my five stories (8, 12, 16, 20, and 24 years), they each revealed the importance of having these five traits in my life as I reflected back over the half century of my life. When I have been at my Biggest, these traits have been in my roles. When they were missing, I discovered it was easy to lose my excitement about whatever I was doing. In my relationships, in my roles, and in my life, I work to ensure I can build these traits into what I do. It is up to me to create the connection with these words in anything and everything I do to ensure I bring these unique and powerful traits into my life.

APPLICATION: LIFE-DEFINING WORDS

1. Review your stories and determine which words best reveal the traits that allow you to feel fully alive and engaged.

2. Assess if they are involved in your life, relationships, and work.

3. How do you design these into your day-to-day actions to bring more meaning to everything you do?

DEEP-LEVEL MINING

The six tools that I have discussed are essential for mining on the surface level for the gold that is right in front of you. Deep-level mining is quite different because it is where you find the gems buried deep in your treasure chest. I am going to introduce two powerful tools for this deep-mining process.

BE BIG: THE BIG POWER OF THE BODY

The body completes all the actions. Our bodies are our ultimate resource to get things done, and sometimes our bodies can be the ultimate obstacle that prevents us from taking action. If we can assess how are body has aligned itself, e.g., the accumulation of all our experiences and history, we can begin to understand what is stopping us from becoming Big, and we can even use our body to evoke our Biggest self. This area of focus is overlooked in our society today. The mind is valued over the body. Tremendous amounts of education and training are available at every level of life to increase the capacity of the mind, but there is very little focus on increasing the capacity of the body. As young children, our bodies are critical resources for us to learn and grow. We play to experience and learn about the world. Before long, outside influences begin to shift the emphasis to the mind with little or no attention on the body and its wisdom and knowledge accumulated from millions of years of evolution.

Our U.S. educational system does attempt to keep our bodies active with sports and physical fitness. These programs enhance the body but typically focus only on physical conditioning, ignoring the practices required to leverage the body's inherent intelligence. Today, with our overburdened lifestyle, poor diets, alcohol consumption, and smoking, as well as exposure to many other environmental toxins, combined with the lack of physical practices, we are disconnected, to say the least, from our body and its unstoppable power.

Most people view the body as just an instrument designed to get them from here to there. We take for granted that some of the most insightful wisdom can come from the body as we move freely in the world. Our use of the five senses—taste, smell, touch, hearing, and sight—is in the background instead of in the foreground to help us create the world of our dreams. Our bodies also contain intelligence that allows us to experience the world at a different level. In my work as a somatic coach, I believe that the body has an amazing capacity to self-heal, self-generate, and self-educate. Our bodies have evolved over millions of years to survive and thrive, but that wisdom within each of us typically goes unnoticed and untapped. Some of us can live our entire life without realizing the power of our body. I believe that to be your Biggest, your ability to tap into this power makes all the difference.

YOUR ACTIONS EACH DAY CREATE PATTERNS AND SHAPES IN YOUR BODY, AND THIS BECOMES YOU.

The other beautiful insight is that the body is not fixed. It is constantly changing. In fact, the body replaces some cells every few days, and our body is constantly regenerating itself. This means we have the ability to change built right into our DNA.

We are never stuck. Being stuck is a state of mind, not of body. We can always learn new behaviors by introducing new practices that modify the body. It takes 300 repetitions to build the first level of muscle memory, and it takes 3,000 repetitions for the behavior to become second nature.

One of my former teachers, Richard Strozzi-Heckler, emphasizes, "You are your practices," meaning what you do every day is who you are.

Your actions each day create patterns and shapes in your body, and this becomes you. Therefore, a secret to life is to look at what you do each day. Introduce new practices with a meaningful story of what you want; then practice the new behavior for 21 days, and you will start to see changes. This is a simple explanation, I agree, but try it and see. Change your practices, change your life!

BECOMING BIG IN THE BODY

There are many practices to show up Big, Bold, and Bad with the body. I will focus on a couple of these throughout the book. While coaching, I always introduce one core practice as a foundation piece for the work with the body. This practice I learned from Strozzi Institute and is available to each of us for anything and everything we do. It is so powerful that it can help you in your relationships and with your career, or help you to be more confident about who you are. I call it "leadership presence."

In the business world, executives often encounter challenges that have no answers. A senior executive shared that when an issue or challenge boils up to the level where it lands on his desk, it is a big, nasty, messy problem without answers. If there were answers, employees in the lower level of the organization—from the frontline worker, to the manager, to the director, to the vice president—would have handled it. In today's world, there is no right or wrong, only uncertainty and speculation about what will happen in the marketplace. When setting a direction for their company, CEOs have to rely on their intuition. Don't get me wrong, they do ask their teams and confidants to provide all the relevant assessments, but the ultimate skill is to allow the body to guide them instinctively on how to move forward. We know some executives miss the mark, and they pay the consequences, but some have instincts right on target.

True skill is to **use the body to provide guidance and direction when the situation is uncertain.** There is a story about the CEO of Sony. His practice was to collect all the assertions and assessments from his team, swallow them, and digest them into his system before he went to bed. In the morning, if he woke up with indigestion, he would not go forward with the project. If he woke up feeling well, he would approve the project.

So you are saying you are not a CEO? Yes, but the reality is you are the CEO of your life. How clear is the future for you? If you are like most people, the future is uncertain. So how do you set a course or make decisions to go forward? The key is tapping into the wisdom of the body.

This exercise will begin to build the connection and awareness with your body. You will begin to tap into some of the subtle, yet powerful insights that are available to you through the body. You will go through three levels of learning as you take on this or any new practice. They are:

1. Familiarity—We have heard about it, or it sounds similar to something we have seen or done before, but we have no other education or training on the subject. This can be a dangerous place because we may believe we got it since it seems familiar, but in reality, we have no clue.

2. Understanding—We have developed a deeper level of insight about the subject. We may have done some reading, coursework, or even some practices to move it into the body, but we are still beginners. The danger here is that we think we got this, yet we are still winging it.

3. Embodiment—We have spent the time, energy, and effort to practice the action. We have done it so many times that it has become part of who we are. Because it is embodied, we can become more open and creative in the process versus trying to figure it out.

With all these newly introduced tools and routines, the more you move toward embodiment, the more value you will receive from this book.

The exercise to build basic awareness of executive presence around your body can be done while you are standing, sitting, lying down, or even moving. In the book entitled *Anatomy of Change*, by Richard Strozzi-Heckler, the author brings forth a powerful interpretation around our body's length, width, and depth. I will share my interpretations of this work, yet I strongly recommend picking up his book and exploring this concept and somatic coaching at a deeper level, www.strozziinstitutue.com.

Here are the steps to developing an executive presence:

We are three-dimensional beings. When we look at our bodies, we have the following dimensions: **length, width** and **depth.**

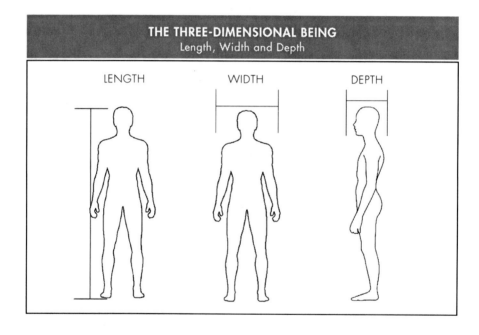

THE THREE-DIMENSIONAL BEING
Length, Width and Depth

LENGTH   WIDTH   DEPTH

Each dimension can bring unique insights to allow us to be more effective. When we are aligned and centered into the wholeness of our body, the wisdom of millions of years of evolution becomes accessible. Being Big in the world requires us to leverage one of the most important tools—our bodies.

Before you proceed on to the exercise to develop your leadership presence, here is a quick summary of what is available to us via our three-dimensional body:

LENGTH

Length is the vertical dimension of the body. Length is the line that runs from head to toe. The wisdom of length enhances our life when we extend the line into the heavens above and ground it into the earth beneath our feet. Our body is the conduit between Heaven and Earth, and if we develop our understanding of length, we can tap into those powerful perspectives. Standing tall in our length gives us the vision to see what others cannot see; we can see across the horizon for what is ahead. Have you ever seen a powerful leader with his head down or not at his full length? Extending your length upwards allows you to tap into the inspiration from above. It's the heavenly inspiration that is not of this world that allows us to see beyond our life and world. Extending your length upwards makes you fearless in the face of challenges in your life because it is a position of great courage and alertness.

Length has two poles. Length is also about extending our energy down into Mother Earth—a nurturing, grounding force that will support our life. There are a couple of key factors about this pole. By staying grounded in length, we will be prevented from floating away in our lofty ideas and fantasies. Furthermore, staying grounded in length allows us a place to discharge our excess energy. Most electrical wall outlets are set up with a ground wire that disperses an overload of electricity into the earth to prevent the outlet from blowing up. We can leverage this same resource in our life. By staying connected to this aspect of length, we can release excess energy (stress) into the ground.

 EXERCISE:

1. As a simple exercise, stand to your full length right now. Extend your length upward by standing tall. At the same time, ground your feet into the floor and imagine roots extending into the earth.

2. What shows up for you as you stand in your full expression of length?

WIDTH

Width is the horizontal plane that surrounds our body. Imagine a Hula-Hoop floating around your waist. Its reach is as big as you want to make the hoop expand. This ring of energy is called the social dimension of our three-dimensional body. It allows us to connect to people, pets (animals), and planet. Through our width, we can connect to one person or connect to thousands or millions. Great leaders have mastered this dimension. Have you viewed a leader or performer from a distance and left feeling they were connected to you? The power of width is amazing. As you begin the practice of width, you will see where you unconsciously pull back your width or where you allow it to flow big. You will also realize it is your choice on how to connect to others, whether it is having a one-on-one engagement or speaking in front of a crowd.

 EXERCISE:

We can begin to access this dimension with the following exercise.

1. Stand tall in your length and begin to open your body.

2. Open your chest area.

3. Pull back your shoulders and allow your arms to extend downward.

4. Slightly open your hands to the front.

5. Expand your stance to be wider than your shoulders.

6 Expand your peripheral vision.

7. Imagine the Hula-Hoop width expanding outward.

Now consider the following questions:
▸ What does this feel like for you?
▸ Can you expand your energy to fill the room?

DEPTH

Depth is the front and back side of the body. This dimension reveals insights about our future and the past. Our front is oriented to our future and where we are going. Our back gives us access to our past experiences and where we have been. Both are critically important to who we are as humans. There are a few challenges to be examined. The first is a strong orientation toward the future. Our body actually leans forward, which can produce a view of the world that forsakes the past or an out-of-balance effect that can result in you figuratively falling on your face. The next challenge would be a strong orientation to the past. The body leans back, actually pulling away. When we are pulling away, we are stuck in a story of the past, which takes over and makes us forsake the present.

The dimension of depth holds tremendous power. The past can serve as a support for us if we allow it. Imagine two hands supporting your back as you tackle new situations. Your past experiences have "got your back" so to speak and can empower you. Use this to your advantage.

 EXERCISE:

We can begin to access this dimension with the following exercise.

1. Stand in your length and width. Now begin to sense your back and front.

2. Rock onto your toes and then rock onto your heels. Finally settle in the perfect balance between the two.

3. Do the same with your head and chest. Rock back and forth, finding the balance between the two.

Now consider the following:

Imagine a future that excites you and pulls you forward. Now see if you can pull back to that perfect balance position between your future and past.

> ‣ Bring your body to a centered position in the present.
> ‣ Do the same for a past story that pulls you back.
> ‣ What does it take to regain the balanced position in your depth?

These three dimensions offer a power that can enhance your ability to Be Big, Bold, and Bad. When you employ all three of these dimensions, you are creating a leadership presence allowing these powerful insights to flow into and through you. Note: The core center of the human body is approximately 2 inches below your belly button. Visualize this as the intersection point for all three dimensions to come together within you. When you are perfectly aligned in the full expression of this practice, you are fully aligned with the power of the body.

EXERCISE: LEADERSHIP PRESENCE

To create a leadership presence, practice the following in front of a mirror. Use the mirror to help you fine-tune your presence as you align around length, width, and depth.

Stand in front of a mirror and observe your length, width, and depth. How does your body look currently in terms of its length, width, and depth?

> ‣ **Length:** Now take a deep breath and align your body to its full length. Extend the vertical line of your body both upward to the sky and downward into the earth. What has to happen in your body to be in the full expression of length?
>
> ‣ **Width:** Take another deep breath and open up your body to be in the dimension of width. Move your feet farther apart, open up your chest, and turn your

hands outward. Your body will feel more open and able to receive. Also feel what it is like to extend your energy outward from this place. What do you have to do to have your energy expand beyond your body and fill the room?

▸ Depth: Take another deep breath and open up your body to feel the dimension of depth. Begin to bring to your conscious mind your back and all the history that lives in this side of depth. Next bring your attention to your front and the powerful orientation to the future. Balance yourself perfectly between your front and back as you stand. Ensure you are not leaning forward or pulling back as you stand.

Take a few deep breaths, and quickly take yourself again through the dimension of length, width, and depth alignment. What feelings, emotions, or sensations are showing up for you when you are standing in your leadership presence?

This is a powerful way to build a deep awareness of your body. By assessing how you feel, your emotions, and sensations, you are strengthening the communication channel between the mind and the body. This in turn will allow the body's intuition, its whispers, to be heard more readily over time.

APPLICATION: THE BIG POWER OF THE BODY

1. Practice aligning your body into the dimensions of length, width, and depth daily.

2. As you align your body, add the following language to enhance the learning and retention;

a. Length (upward)— *I am a leader with great visions, and I receive heavenly inspiration.*

b. Length (downward)— *I am grounded in life. I can release my excess energy into the earth.*

c. Width— *I am connected. My energy extends beyond my body and can influence others.*

d. Depth— *I am perfectly aligned between the wisdom of my past and the potential of my future.*

3. Begin to practice your leadership presence in front of others. What reactions do you receive?

4. What situations make you contract and get small in your length, width, and depth? Practice being aware of those situations and use this leadership presence to realign your length, width, and depth.

5. Begin to observe where your intuition, insights, and awareness increase as you practice leadership presence daily.

YOUR PERSONAL HISTORY: INSIGHTS & UNDERSTANDING

"If you don't know history, then you don't know anything.
You are a leaf that doesn't know it is part of a tree."
—Michael Crichton—

Our history is like the roots of a tree. Deep roots allow us to scale to our highest level because they are a solid foundation that can hold us and provide the essential nutrients for our good growth. Looking back at our history allows us to design actions for going forward. History is a secret weapon with its powerful intelligence about what has shaped us for both good and bad. In the book entitled *The Art of War*, by Sun Tzu, the first and foremost key to winning a battle is having greater intelligence. According to Tzu, "If you know the enemy and you know yourself, you need not fear the results of a hundred battles." We are in an age of information, yet the information that is available to us is overwhelming. This information is not intelligence. The abundant amount of outside information is meaningless unless we craft our own meaning and significance from it.

The secret weapon is to know yourself, and this, unfortunately, cannot be achieved with a Google search! It requires a search of your own archives to reveal the treasures and landmarks of your past. This will help you design the strategy that aligns with your Bigness.

In this Be Big section, you are discovering the roots of your tree. You have used several exercises to see how you are set up to engage with the outside world in the most powerful way, your Biggest way! This is, as I mentioned, unique to each of us. The unique mixture of all these makes us a force that is Big and powerful. Digging into your past is the last piece needed to "find the gold and release the old."

In the following exercise, I am going to discuss your history—the stories you built—using a tool called "language." Language was invented so we can build a better understanding of what we perceive and communicate more effectively with others. We sometimes fail to understand that creating our stories does not make them the truth. It is our opinion of what is happening, and if you think about it, there are thousands of other ways to interpret what is happening to you or what is happening right in front of you. There are many examples we see in life to prove this. One ground rule to hold in this process is that there are no right or wrong interpretations. There are just more powerful ones. Therefore, your ability to create new interpretations or be open to new ones is where you begin the powerful dance of seeing new possibilities.

My opinion is that if we get fixed in how we view the world, then we are asking for trouble. An example is a simple story we might create about a pen. Is a pen really a pen? If I were to hold up a pen in my hand and ask you what it is, your automatic answer would be that it is a pen. And if I ask you if you would be willing to bet $1,000 on it, you would probably accept. Heck, your certainty is grounded in the recurrence over a lifetime of using a pen. A pen is a pen; no ifs, ands, or buts, right? If that same "pen" is repositioned in my hand, and I held it like a dagger then asked you what it is, if you were to say that it is a pen, then you might be in serious danger. Because in my mind, it is now a weapon, and because of your certainty, you cannot even envision the new possibility until it is too late. Watch a James Bond or a Jason Bourne spy movie to see how a pen is never a pen. That begs the question: Is what we perceive right in front of us really the truth?

Therefore, in this exercise, the value is to challenge your language and interpretation about your stories. They are not real or fixed. They are just an interpretation that at the time best served you. We sometimes perceive situations from a skewed or outdated perspective, and this is where the value of this exercise lies. It lies in your ability to find another way to view this situation to empower more meaning in your life. *Please note: this exercise is about looking for new ways to move forward in life through your own very personal challenges, finding a new meaning, and building new interpretations that may better serve you on your quest to Be Big, Bold and Bad.*

 EXERCISE: PERSONAL HISTORY—MEMORY REFLECTION

This reflection process is critical for this Be Big section. It allows you to access deeply archived thoughts that reveal themselves as you open memories of your history. Trust yourself to find and reveal what is important even if you cannot make sense of why that memory showed up. The memories you recall can be positive or challenging. There is no right or wrong in this exercise. Spend 60 minutes at a minimum in this reflection. Find a quiet time in your day when your energy is high and creative. Please engage in this exercise with a mood of being curious and interested in revisiting your powerful history.

1. Prepare a list of your top 15 to 20 life-impacting moments. The list can be in an outline format or a longer written response.

2. Please reflect back to the beginning of your life and walk through your early history. My recommendation is to spend the majority of your time reflecting on your youth, ages 1 to 16.

3. Reflect on life-impacting moments that happened from ages 1 to 5, 6 to 10, 11 to 16, etc. I have found that these early experiences set us up for how the rest of our life plays out. Later "life-impacting" moments are typically (but not always) experienced based on the shaping and common sense we received early in our life.

APPLICATION: PERSONAL HISTORY—MEMORY REFLECTION

We are going to look at this from a high level. This exercise can reveal a tremendous amount about who you are, how you view the world, and why that is so. We will focus on a few examples. It will be up to you to dig deeper into more of your own personal history.

1. Review your reflections of your life-impacting moments from the list you created in the previous exercise, and follow this process.

   a. Pick one moment which seems to call out to you and has a challenging association with who you are today.

b. Write in your journal the detailed story about what happened or talk into a recorder about this life-impacting story. This interpretation is your reality about what happened. Yet is it true?

We use language to reveal our views and make sense of it all, but our story about the situation is not necessarily the truth. It is just our singular view at one moment.

1. Listen to the recording and take notes about the parts of your story you feel could be reinvented, or where a new story could help you "find the gold and release the old."

2. Invent a new perspective. Look at the language you use to describe the situation.
   a. Does the language empower or limit you?
   b. Is there another way to describe this situation using more empowering words?

3. Look at the situation you picked from these three different points of view.
   a. Yours: How else could you see it that would better serve you?
   b. Theirs: Put yourself in the other person's point of view. How would you then describe it?
   c. Higher Power's: Put it in the higher power's point of view. Assume that it is always for good.

4. Now choose another significant event and follow the same format listed above.

This is a powerful process to look at events which have shaped you emotionally. They are your top moments, so their impact is real to you. Yet as you can see with this exercise, every situation can be seen from different points of view.

The outcome of this exercise is to find the moments of your past that enhance you, and to bring more light and energy to them. Then, find the moments from your past that shut you down and make you small, and reinvent the meaning and language so they have little or no influence over you as we go forward.

BE BIG: WRAP UP

This Be Big section was about discovering some of your unique gifts you bring to your everyday life. These insights about you will be the foundation for the work going forward. As we discussed, awareness is a key part of being present and powerful in today's marketplace which is constantly shifting and changing. Knowing who you are helps you to design the actions you will need to ensure you are travelling on the path to your Biggest self. I have included a high level worksheet in the back of the book to capture each of the eight insights you have learned from the exercises so they can be readily accessible for your reference in this process. This is just the first step of your discovery process about who you are, how you were shaped, and what unique skills and talents you alone bring to the table. I would encourage you to continue to explore other assessment tools so you can always be enhancing your awareness about who you are. There is an abundance of gold within you. Keep prospecting!

THREE

———————

BE BOLD

Being Bold is *showing an ability to take risks, to be confident, and to be courageous.* This section is going to take you on an internal journey of first being Bold with yourself. You'll face and eliminate some of the challenges that slow you down; build a Bold stand in the world using your body as the instrument of power; and create a template that serves as a guidepost to bring out and maintain your Badass. You will learn a new conversational tool to empower more effective action with others, clean up your old patterns, step up your skills around being effective with others, and Be Bold by having faith that you are on a bigger journey than you can imagine.

One of the reasons I am so drawn to my work is how I can quickly discover the root of an issue and then shift the meaning to bring about a significant change for the client. To illustrate, I worked with an executive client who had sold his successful start-up. The sale afforded him the time to step back for a bit. Now, he was hunting for a new executive-level role. During our first meeting, I listened to his language as he described how he was networking ineffectively. I asked him the best open-ended question in the book, "WHY?" He said he did not feel confident talking to people because he was in a place of need. He had not maintained his network and felt guilty about re-engaging people, as if he would be taking advantage of them. This feeling was the barrier.

When I work with someone, I listen first to their language as they describe what is happening. I continue the questioning until I see the restrictive box that they have built with their language. For Mr. X, his language revealed a story that was limiting his action of networking. "I cannot network because I ignored my network; if I ask for help now, I will be taking from others, and the equation will be out of balance." The first step was to look at the story and offer him new language, e.g., stories that open up new possibilities or ways to empower him to take action. I asked, "When someone asks you for help, do you help? If yes, how does that make you feel?" He said he does help, and he enjoys the opportunity to do so. Then I told him, "Can you see how asking for help is actually a way to help others?" Sometimes reinterpreting someone's story can change a behavior, but typically this is not enough to create lasting change. With Mr. X, I could see that he was still concerned about "taking" from others. He said, "Everyone is so busy, and I have not maintained the relationships, so I don't see how I could re-engage my network." I began to take him to a lower level of understanding. I took him out of his language, out of his mind, and into his body.

I asked him to stand and take a few deep breaths, then I took him through the executive presence exercise I described in the previous Be Big section. I walked him through the length, width, and depth dimensions, and then guided him through a muscle-relaxing exercise. The purpose was to get him out of his head and into his body, so we could access his internal wisdom. Shifting to this state is a key ingredient to getting people to go to a deeper level. The mind is a powerful tool which will dominate if we do not have the tools and practices to ease the mind from its influence over us.

I asked him to shut his eyes and take a couple more deep breaths. I asked him to tell me where the story he told me lives in the body. That is an unusual question, but our bodies are a reservoir for all our experiences, and being able to isolate where the issue lies within us is critical. I asked him again. He sorted through his body and pointed to the top of his head, right front side. Now that we had isolated the story, we wanted to define it and make it something real that he could deal with versus just a feeling. I asked him if he could associate an image to the feeling. He was quiet for a moment and then said it is a burglar—the cartoon-type burglar with a black-striped outfit and mask. I asked him clarifying questions to make it even more concrete and then more questions to determine how he could get rid of it. He began to feel a connection between his heart and the spot on his head.

In this work, there are always deeper layers. The deeper we can go, the more success we can have with the issue. As I asked him to breathe into his heart, another story spontaneously revealed itself. He was not sure why this story came out, but I knew this was the body wisdom speaking to us. As a kid, he was caught taking some candy from a store. The embarrassment was terrible when he had to face his parents. He

CHANGE ONLY HAPPENS WHEN WE HAVE OUR EMOTIONS INVOLVED.

reported that the emotion of shame was overwhelming. Here was the root cause from five decades ago that lived deep in his body and affected his entire being. I followed the same process of discovering what image was associated with the feeling of shame in his heart. He breathed into the heart area, calling up all of the old feelings, and told me he saw a brick wall. I questioned him a bit to make it more real. Now we could deal with the constriction that was the brick wall protecting his heart from the feeling of shame anytime he felt he was taking something. It was time to change his association and to generate the energy and emotions to destroy the wall. Change only happens when we have our emotions involved.

I questioned him a few times around the problems, issues, and pains this brick wall was causing in his life. I wanted to ensure he was energized, or "mad as Hell, and not going to take this anymore," and ready to destroy that damn brick wall. I asked him what was the best way to destroy a brick wall, and he came up with a bulldozer, a big one. I began to help him visualize the bulldozer with questions to create the image in his head. I then walked him through the imagery of climbing into the bulldozer and starting the engine. I asked him to set the front plow in the right position to knock down this wall of shame. He took control and knocked down the wall. I asked him to describe what was on the other side. "Expansive space and freedom," he said. I asked him to back up and run over the debris, and then look down and tell me what he saw. "I see red and gray dust from pulverized bricks." I asked him to associate a feeling to this new space without a wall and to imagine what he could do now that the old restrictive story was no longer in his heart. We wrapped up the visualization, and I asked him to open his eyes. He became very excited about the process and got into a new frame of mind about networking and asking for help from others.

This work is transformational, and it is available to anyone willing to push the edges of how they understand their world. It focuses on one of our most fundamental systems—our biology. We are built to survive. It is our first instinct. As a child, our body relies heavily on the love and protection of our parents. If any type of situation occurred to us as a child in which our relationship with our parents was threatened, our body would have stepped in to ensure it never happened again. The bigger the emotional outlay, the deeper it is rooted to the point where we do not even know it is the reason for our actions as adults. I speculate that once we leave the safety of our home and parents, most of us never examine how our life experiences under our parents or caregiver shaped us to REACT. We continue to move in the world as if all the situations we encounter as adults are the same as when we were children.

Our society, as far as I can tell, does not provide the education or training to help people become aware of these automatic behaviors. We are not trained to see that we do have choices—lots of choices. Thus, we create automatic reaction narratives that help us justify our thinking that we are okay and others are wrong. A great way to get out of your automatic reaction is to tell yourself, "If I point one finger at another, I should be pointing three fingers back at myself." In other words, the issue is three times more likely to be your issue than somebody else's.

 EXERCISE: MOOD CHECK

Becoming aware of our moods can help us choose how we want to see the world. A mood check at this stage in the book will help you determine your progress and the effects of the exercises on you.

1. What is your mood now?
2. Did anything about this work or outside this work trigger you into your current mood?
3. Is that the optimum mood for this work?
4. Can you change it to a more powerful mood?
5. How will you make the change?

BE BOLD: FACE AND ELIMINATE YOUR BRICK WALLS

In this next section of Be Bold, **the process will take courage.** This section is all about stepping up and facing the transformation you have to undergo to free yourself of the deep-rooted, limiting beliefs that live inside you. This process is best done with the help of someone trained in this area, but the premise of this book is to provide the tools and resources you need to enable you to guide yourself into being Big, Bold, and Bad. I also believe that our bodies have the capacity to self-heal, self-educate, and self-generate. Just look how wonderfully this complex mind, body, and spirit function without any conscious attention. For instance, I am not asking my body to breathe or my heart to pump; it just does so to ensure I stay alive and healthy. Who says our body is not ready to purge the limiting beliefs by itself? Just open the door and get out of the way. The following exercises will open the door. The rest requires you to step courageously into the past, discover old patterns that are no longer useful in your life, and acknowledge them for their service and support. Let them go; they are no longer needed.

 EXERCISE: FACE AND ELIMINATE YOUR BRICK WALLS

1. Journal areas in your life where you face challenges.

2. Pick just one area from your list to begin the process. For example, in the past I used to have an issue in the corporate world with being around senior male leaders in the organization. I wrote down the challenge, "Why do I avoid meetings or interactions with senior male leaders, like CEOs and other executives?"

3. Become more aware of what impact this challenge is having on your life. Bring in some emotions around the challenge. Build emotions that will serve as a charge to bust through the challenge. Ask yourself these questions:
   a. What is not happening in your life?
   b. What is it costing you in your relationships, career, and life? (For example, I was purposely pulling back from projects and meetings to ensure I stayed out of the direct line of sight of the CEO. This cost me career advancement and potential income).

4. Find where this challenge lives in your body.
   a. Find a quiet place to connect to your body for 20 minutes.

b. Stand up and do the executive presence exercise from the Be Big section to get you out of your head and into your body.

c. Sit down in that state and close your eyes. Take a few deep breaths, and begin to ask yourself where the challenge lives in your body. A good rule of thumb is "first thought is best thought" in this exercise. Once you identify the spot, touch the spot with your hand. *(For example, I found it in my heart, as a tightening.)*

5. Make it real to you.

   Now that you have located the challenge in your body, it is time to make it easier to identify. Begin to describe it.

   ‣ Can you identify it as an object of some type?

   ‣ What pictures pop into your mind that signify the challenge in your body?

   ‣ What size is it?

   ‣ How deep is it?

   ‣ What color is it?

   (For example, I visualized my constriction as a medium-sized white towel that was wound up tightly, as if someone had been trying to wring out its last drop of water.)

6. Find the meaning.

   a. This location is holding a story you have from the past that causes the challenge you identify.

   b. Take a deep breath; enter into the location; and with your eyes closed, envision what caused the pain. What happened in your life that resulted in the action you mentioned in question one?

    c. What stories are you holding about what happened to you that you have not let go?

    (For example, in my reflection, I discovered that I was staying under the radar of powerful men because that is the strategy I adopted in my family. I was raised by a strict father who was the son of a policeman in the 1930s and '40s. In my father's household and ours, there was a hard line about right and wrong, and the consequences were serious if someone crossed the line. Therefore, as a young boy, I learned to stay under my dad's radar. This under-the-radar strategy showed up throughout my life—in my social circles and at work—until I went through this exercise.)

6. Get ready to take action to change your life.

    a. We now know where it lives, what it looks like, and why it is there. Now we need to build the energy to eradicate it from its deep armored bunker.

    b. Revisit number two above, and continue to build the story of why this is no longer useful in your life.

    c. You need to tell yourself, "I will never go back to that behavior; it does not serve me anymore. It hurts my relationships, my career, and my life."

    d. It is time for you to move through this once and for all.

    ▸ When I discovered my story about my actions to protect myself as a child, I realized this strategy was no longer necessary. Heck, I was a 40-year-old man! I was no longer a little boy. I started to see all the places where I had pulled back in life, in relationships, and in the world to stay under the radar. Then I developed the energy around not letting this hold me back any more. I had to change. I was no longer going to walk around all wound up and ringed out, protecting myself.

7. Taking action to change/eradicate the issue.
   a. Enter into a centered state by doing the executive presence exercise. Take several deep breaths, and get the body charged and ready to serve you. Then imagine the picture of the contraction in your body. Paint a vivid picture with all the details. Make it as real as possible.
   b. Using Big energy, tell yourself the stories of why you no longer need this in your body. It no longer serves your purpose, and you no longer want to live and adjust your life to accommodate this old story and pattern.
   c. Now that your system is charged, streaming with energy to eradicate this limiting belief, ask yourself, **"What is the best tool I can use to eliminate this from my life and destroy its power over me?"** In the earlier example, my client used a bulldozer. Sometimes it can be as simple as untying the knot in your stomach. The body will provide the appropriate solution to deal with the obstruction when you ask the right question.
   d. Take the tool and do the deed. This is a critical step to allow you to experience the dismantling and destruction of your unique limiting belief. Manage every detail of the process until you completely eradicate it. Spare no expense in using your creativity to finish the job. Bring all hands on deck to fight the battle. Destroy it!

▸ In my client's story, the bulldozer demolished the brick wall and then ran over the brick rubble repeatedly until it was dust. In my story, the white towel was wound up so tightly that the twist was becoming twisted upon itself. When I asked myself which tool I should use to release the twist, the answer was simple. Just unwind the twist. Slowly, I saw the towel releasing each twist until the towel was a flat, open, expansive space.

APPLICATION: LOCKING IT IN

Now that you have taken care of the image, make sure you have the story and practices in place to ensure it does not come back. You will want to prevent it from rebuilding itself from the rubble.

1. You need to lock in a new story that emotionally connects you to the new behavior and feeling.
   a. What does it feel like now that the contraction is gone?
   b. What is available now that was not even visible before?
   c. What can you accomplish now to change your life for the better?

2. Next, you need to introduce practices to support the new pattern.
   a. High intensity affirmations help us lock in the behavior.
   b. Check into the area and reinforce that it no longer exists.
   c. Take actions that you would not have taken before and celebrate your growth and change.
   d. Enlist others in your process, and ask them to help you stay accountable through your first steps of change.

> This is the powerful new beginning for you. It is time to let go of all those limiting beliefs you have been holding in your body. Be Bold!

BE BOLD: USE YOUR BRAIN TO SUPPORT YOUR NEW PATH

I was listening to National Public Radio on a long car ride home from Los Angeles, and the conversation focused on how the brain works. The speaker used an analogy that brought some clarity to my understanding. If your brain were Google, then the conscious brain is like Google's home page—a very thin interface not designed for major input or computations. Its simple purpose is to access the major archives of data—our subconscious mind. He explained when we ask our brain questions, it searches our subconscious archives for the response. The brain does not care what question we ask it. It has no judgment or criteria about whether the answer will best serve you. It just answers the question. This is where most of us misuse the power of one of our best resources. If we want to Be Big, Bold, and Bad, we must be careful which questions we ask our own personal Google home page, our conscious mind. A simple question not phased correctly could surface many answers that do not serve us. Here is a question you might have asked yourself: "Why is my life not working out?" You have activated the system to seek the reason why your life will not work out. And believe me, these types of questions bring back a slew of answers to bring you down further, which then will provoke more bad questions. As I discussed earlier, our language reveals our world to others, and yes, it even shapes our world by influencing our brains to work against us. The key to remember: the kind of questions you seed in your brain will build you up or pull you down. It is your choice. To Be Bold is to enlist the brain in a positive and powerful way to serve your greater purpose and calling.

EXERCISE: USING THE BRAIN

The brain's power is always available to each of us. Let us use it to our advantage. Challenge yourself today to ask your brain the right questions, and stop the questions that send you in the wrong direction.

1. For the next week, keep track of the questions you are seeping into your brain.

2. Review your questions you have been asking yourself at the end of the week.

3. Which ones were empowering? Which ones were not?

4. Can you rewrite your questions to bring you the answers you are looking for?

5. Can you recognize a pattern in the questions you ask yourself?

6. Is there one key question you ask yourself constantly?

 APPLICATION: USING THE BRAIN

1. What is one bold question you can ask yourself now to support this new journey? Be Bold and allow your powerful brain to do its magic.

2. Pay attention to the questions you are conditioned to ask yourself. Practice reframing them to seek out positive outcomes.

3. Be Bold and choose to ignore the noise of life that clouds your brain with information that supports the dark side.

4. Ask yourself, "How can I be even more Big, Bold, and Bad in everything I do?"

BE BOLD: CONVERSATION FOR ACTION

In 1994 during some coursework with an organization, Hecht and Associates, a map was introduced to the group, entitled "Conversation for Action." The originators of the chart were Fernando Flores and Terry Winograd. The map was created from their work while writing the book entitled *Understanding Computers and Cognition.* The map has proven to be a pivotal tool for effective conversations with my clients and others. I have it here in the Be Bold section because working with this map requires a rigor about life, your time, and your relationships. If you follow a certain process, the map will provide a fundamental look at how conversations are constructed. There is tremendous depth in what can be learned when using this map. To become Bold in your conversations is to ensure that you coordinate effectively in every request and promise you use.

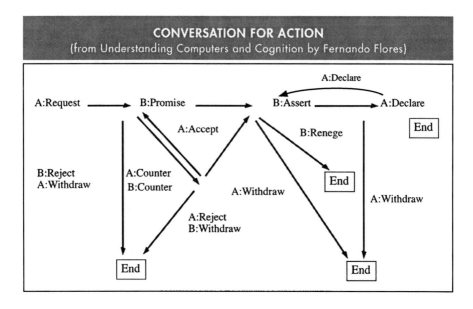

CONVERSATION FOR ACTION
(from Understanding Computers and Cognition by Fernando Flores)

At first glance, the chart may appear a bit confusing, but I will break it down into a few simple and powerful interpretations to leverage its power in conversations.

BE **BAD**!

The top line outlines how action conversations are constructed:

REQUEST > PROMISE > ASSERT > DECLARE

For this exercise, the definitions of these four elements are:

A. **Request:** to formally ask for something.

B. **Promise:** a commitment that something will happen.

C. **Assert:** to state something in a strong, definite way.

D. **Declare:** to make something known or formal.

Let us look at the first two parts of the map:

1. REQUEST > PROMISE

It appears simple, but we sometimes ignore the important ingredients of a request likely because we do not know the essentials. Here is an example to demonstrate how it can get complicated. The Requester makes a request: *Will you go to coffee with me?* The Promiser says, *Yes.* Simple, but what is missing with the request? Here is where most conversations can fail. What is missing is **When, Where,** and **Why.**

An appropriate request requires the following:
- **When:** Will you go to coffee with me tomorrow at noon?
- **Where:** Let's meet at Starbucks on North Santa Cruz Blvd. in Los Gatos, next to Petco.
- **Why:** I want to discuss project XYZ and the next set of deliverables.

As you can see, the Requester has set the stage for the Promiser to fully understand the request and to be able to determine if they can fulfill that promise. When Requester or Promiser make assumptions about this critical information, they are both opening themselves up for a conversation that produces no action, or worse, the wrong action. When we make ASSumptions, we run the risk of being the ASS.

Once an appropriate request is made, the Promiser, who fully understands the request, assesses if he can accommodate the request to fulfill the promise. If he accepts and makes the promise, then the second half of the chart becomes relevant.

2. ASSERT > DECLARE

Assert means the Promiser tells the Requester that he has completed the request as specified. Once this is asserted, it is up to the Requester to either accept the assertion that the request is completed as specified, or declare that the request was not completed as specified and ask him to do it again.

Declare means to accept or not accept the assertion of the Promiser that the work is complete. This is a vital part of closing the loop in a conversation. Many conversations are left open because the Requester did not take the final step. It can produce dissatisfaction in the Promiser because he completed the task yet does not know if the job is done or meets the approval of the Requester. It is critical to close conversation loops for both parties.

EXERCISE: CONVERSATION FOR ACTION

Here are a few steps to incorporate into your daily life using this Conversation for Action map. I will also include a few points about the lower half of the map.

1. Start by mapping out your current conversations.
   a. Are you making the right requests?
   b. Are you making promises you can keep?
   c. Are you asserting on time and to specification?
   d. Are you closing the loop on all conversations and declaring you are satisfied or not?
   e. Where do your conversations break down?

2. Start to practice being more rigorous around all four stages of the chart.

   a. Requester: Make great requests using When, Where, and Why.

   b. Promiser: Ensure you fully understand the request. No ASSumptions.

   c. Assert: Do not let your promises miss the mark; assert on time and to the specifications.

   d. Declare: This is a critical step for the promise and request. Always close the loop.

3. Now start to look at the lower half of chart:

   a. Leverage your ability to counter-offer.
      ‣ Requester: Be open-minded to a conversation to clarify a request or change it if required.
      ‣ Promiser: The only time to negotiate is prior to making a promise. There is no backing out once the promise is made without serious consequences.

   b. Consequences of withdrawal.
      ‣ Promiser: When we break promises, people will pull back in making future requests of us.
      ‣ Requester: When we withdraw our requests, people will stop making promises to fulfill on our requests.

   c. Consequences of Renege.
      ‣ When a Promiser reneges, they reveal their focus is on themselves without a concern for the commitment to the requester.
      ‣ When you renege, you lose the trust of the requester, and future requests will not take place.

APPLICATION—CONVERSATION FOR ACTION

1. Post this chart in your office or where you spend much of your day.

2. Look at it daily. If you fail, find out where you fail, and declare a new practice to change your behavior.

3. Be Bold around the conversation you are in. Your time, identity, and relationships are on the line.

BE BOLD: TAKE A STAND

What does it mean to TAKE A STAND? I opened this book up with a scene from the movie Network. In the scene a newscaster took a stand for what he believed, and he empowered others to do the same using a rally cry, "Get up and go to the window and yell out, I am mad as Hell, and I am not going to take this anymore."

Taking a stand can be defined as:

‣ Adopting a firm position about an issue.
‣ Holding one's ground against the enemy.
‣ Taking action; standing up for oneself.

I have seen in myself and in my clients how valuable the ability to take a stand is. However, most of us do not take stands unless we are pushed to our limits. These next three definitions encompass the power of what taking a stand will bring to you in all areas of your life.

1. Taking a stand will keep you grounded around issues that you face, both small and large.

2. Taking a stand will allow you to fend off "the enemy," both internally and externally.

3. Taking a stand allows you to take actions to show up in your Biggest, Boldest, and most Badass self.

Taking a stand seems so obvious. Although we have a basic understanding, it does not mean we actually have developed this skill enough for it to become a valuable resource for us to deploy in every aspect of our life.

There are key components that make up an effective stand:

▸ **We must have a clear focus of what we are taking a stand around.** This is a big issue. Most people are willing to float with the outcomes that come their way. They are not clear on their stand around an issue, a competitor, or themselves. This book is about stepping into your unstoppable power and knowing your stand.

▸ **We must have the practices in place to support our stand:**
There are three types of practices we need to employ:

1. The first practice is to be able to articulate your stand in language. People need to know what you are all about. Your ability to practice this and to see where your language is inconsistent with your stand is step one. Step two is articulating your stand in a way people can understand. Simplicity is key.

2. The second practice is to embody the stand in your entire being. It is easy to talk the talk, but can you walk the walk? When you speak, are you grounded in your presence? Are the stands truly congruent with who you are? Can people tell who you are and what you stand for from their first contact with you? This practice lives in the physical side of your body.

3. The third practice is to connect your stand to your higher calling— the reason why you are on this planet. Connect it to your destiny.

You will see the unstoppable power of your stand when you align your mind, body, and spirit. I will introduce several practices to align all three with your stands.

BE BOLD!

We have done a lot of work in the previous Be Big section. These are revealing insights to help you design a "stand" that is consistent and congruent with who you are. There are many areas in your life to take a stand around, and I will use examples to help you build the necessary practices to accomplish your goals. Let us start with taking a stand around your being Big, Bold, and Bad.

Build the "stand" that you are a Badass! I can only imagine the stories that you might dream up as to why this is not true. Believe me, I have used them all over the past few decades. I was a superman underneath but never took off the suit to reveal my super powers. Being Bold means that you are ready to shed the suit and step into your unstoppable power.

You are already a Badass, and this is not a place that is new. It is within you and has surfaced from time to time over your lifetime. We are going to capture that moment and create a template of your

> YOU WILL SEE THE UNSTOPPABLE POWER OF YOUR STAND WHEN YOU ALIGN YOUR MIND, BODY, AND SPIRIT.

Badass that you can practice repeatedly. You are a Badass. Let that in! You are a Badass. You are a Badass. Can you feel the power of that?

Or, are you seeking reasons why you are not? As I discussed earlier, utilizing the brain's ability to seek and find reasons to support you is one key. Let the brain do the deep Google search inside your massive mind and find the reasons why you are a Badass. It all starts with the affirmation "I am a Badass," and the magic of the brain builds the story.

THE EMBODIMENT OF YOUR STAND

What is it like to take a stand physically? Imagine two sumo wrestlers. Each standing their ground in the small circle declaring, "I own this space," but it really comes down to who physically and mentally will take a stronger stand. Who is more present to what is happening? Who is more centered?

Who maintains his ground despite the tremendous force trying to disrupt his stand? Who is clearer on his story and purpose? Most of us look at their appearance as the key factor, but they both have similar strength and weight. So why does one win?

Yes, you are not in a sumo-wrestling ring, but I hope the analogy allows you to see that you are a taking a stand in the world. There are always other opponents inside and outside of you trying to push you out of your ring. These internal and external forces seek to find the weakness in your stand, and they play off those weaknesses to get the advantage. Your victory depends on you to be clear on your stand.

At one of the Tony Robbins events I attended, I participated in an exercise to help develop a powerful view on when you are your best and your worst. I found this exercise insightful and have included my version. I focused on creating a template to reveal when you are your strongest in all the areas of Mind, Body, and Spirit. This template is the start of building a stand to Be Big, Bold and Bad in your ring of life.

TAKING A STAND: YOUR BADASS TEMPLATE—STEP ONE

Write in your journal a situation or time when you felt like a Badass in your journal. Think of a time when you were fully alive, confident, and unstoppable. Sometimes we have to go far back into our past. Sometimes we have to look at our childhood to find out where we were our Biggest and Boldest expression of ourselves. Now that you have the situation in mind, what were the feelings you experienced? It is important to get into the feeling state now. This is where the passion and energy live.

 EXERCISE: CREATE YOUR BADASS TEMPLATE

Close your eyes. Now take a few deep breaths to bring some new energy into your body. Envision the Badass situation again. Recreate it in your mind and body. Let the experience be flooded with the feelings you listed above. Remember all the details of who you were at that time. Continue to breathe deeply and allow the experience to live within you again. Now open your eyes, and answer the following questions to create your unique Badass template. There are three key areas we are going to look at in constructing your Badass template: your Mind, Body, and Spirit. Write down your answers on one page in your journal that you can reference later.

1. The MIND

When we look at the Mind, there are two areas to explore to uncover the key themes associated with your Badass self: Your mindset and your words.

▸ Mindset questions to reveal who you were when you were in the Badass state:
   a. What do I focus on? What do I think about?
   b. What do I BELIEVE about myself?
   c. What do I believe about others and the world?
   d. What do I value?
   e. What are my rules?

▸ Word questions to reveal who you were when you were in the Badass state:
   a. What was I saying to myself?
   b. What was I saying to others?
   c. What would I say to myself to be my Badass self always?
   d. What would I need to remember? (Create affirmations.)

2. The BODY

When we rebuild the Badass body, we want to reveal the shape we held in the body. The body is an amazing organism. It holds our entire life history and experiences. In addition, the body provides intelligence to us from our long evolutionary history and ancestry. The body immediately can remember these experiences and shift our entire being in the moment. For instance, when we stand tall, we become a different person immediately, as we also do when we slump our shoulders. The body can be shaped to produce the outcomes we desire. In Amy Cuddy's TED Talk, "*Your body language shapes who you are*," she indicates the body can be tricked based on how we stand. She says that if we hold a power stance for two minutes, our entire physiology changes. Therefore, we are going to use your body's intelligence to recreate your Badass self. Again, breathe and recreate the Badass situation and feelings you listed above. Now answer the following questions.

› Body/Shape questions to reveal who you were when you were in the Badass state. (*Remember we are creating a template to refer back to any time you want to recreate the Badass you. The more detail about how your body was set up, the better. This is a pattern we want to reveal.*)

   a. How did you move and stand with your body? Describe the characteristics of how your body was shaped.
   b. Describe how you held your chest and shoulders in that moment.
   c. Describe how you held your head.
   d. What type of eye contact was happening?
   e. Describe your breath pattern.
   f. Were your muscles tight or loose?
   g. What was the volume, tone, and pitch of your voice?

3. The SPIRIT

What is your calling? Are there times in your life when you connect to a greater energy? One of the explorations of life we all face at some time is to consider if there is something greater than us. There are many practices in the world that focus on developing this connection. We are going to explore a few questions around how you are destined to show up in your Biggest, Boldest, and Baddest self. Is that too Bold? Of course it is! This is what this book is all about: stretching you beyond what your common sense says is right in order to break down the old barriers and revisit the true power within YOU!

‣ Spirit questions to reveal who you were when you were in the Badass state:

   a. Did you feel connected to a greater force when you were your Biggest, Boldest, and Badass self? Some people call this "flow."

   b. Describe your experience when you are on purpose and in the flow.

APPLICATION: CREATING A BADASS TEMPLATE

   1. Create a Badass template on one page.

   2. Practice reading it daily and building the Mind, Body, and Spirit into your Badass self.

   3. Track your success when you are in your Badass mode. We want to associate good experiences with being a Badass all the time.

   4. Use this template as a foundation for your stand.

BE BOLD: HAVE FAITH IN YOUR DESTINY

Destiny is something which most of us believe in but not at a level where it influences our lives. As I have discussed, language is a way for us to make sense of what is happening in our world. Yet language is limiting, too. In our own mind, we match what is happening outside of us to something that happened to us in the past. We then can make sense of it. Here, we limit our experiences to our mind's capacity, but there is another realm, which is that of the body. We talked about our body earlier and the powerful dimension and intelligence of length, width, and depth. Our body's ability to "sense" the world makes us open to new feelings and experiences. It then instinctively gives us the intelligence to act. The last dimension is beyond our mind and our earthly body; it is outside of us! This is the place where the word "faith" comes into play. Faith I will define as *complete trust or confidence in someone or something, based on a spiritual comprehension rather than proof.* Here is where Be Bold comes into play. How can you trust something you cannot prove? How can you build the belief that something good will come from a situation when all you see is darkness? Being Bold opens us up to a new view of the world, a view that appreciates and allows that our mind and body sometimes do not have the answers, or realizing the only savior may be beyond the understanding of our Mind and Body.

FAITH I WILL DEFINE AS COMPLETE TRUST OR CONFIDENCE IN SOMEONE OR SOMETHING, BASED ON A SPIRITUAL COMPREHENSION RATHER THAN PROOF

Can you step back and say, "I have faith it will work out the way it is meant to be, and whatever happens is the right path for me?"

Here is a great story that opens us up to the possibility that there may be something greater happening beyond our understanding. In a village a man named Peter would frequently visit a church and speak to God. He would kneel down in front of the statue of God and pray. He developed a personal relationship with God and was able to have a two-way conversation. One day, Peter asked God if he could switch places with him for a day and experience the connection and conversations shared with the people who came to the church. God said, "Yes," but with one condition: in no way was he to interfere with anything that may happen. Peter agreed, and the next day he came back to the church. He exchanged places with God and became the statue. Just then, a rich man from the village came to pray and knelt down in front of the statue. He prayed, "Dear God, thank you for providing me with all the bounty and good fortune in my life. The abundance you granted me is amazing. Thank you, God."

He finished and got up to leave. Peter noticed the man had left his billfold full of cash on the pew next to where he was kneeling. However, Peter remembered his promise to God and did nothing. The next person to enter the church was a very poor man from the village. He knelt down in front of the statue and began to pray, "Dear God, thank you for all you have blessed me with. I have a beautiful family, and we are all healthy and happy, but I need to ask for your graces. I am in need of money to care for the education of one of my children. Will you help me to find the resources to provide this opportunity for my child? Thank you, dear God."

Just as he finished, he began to get up and saw the billfold of money sitting on the pew next to him. Immediately he picked it up and praised God for answering his prayer. He then turned and walked away. Peter was taken aback by this action, and he was getting very upset. He was about to do something, but remembered his promise to God and resisted. Another man entered the church. He was a fisherman from the village. He knelt down in front of the statue of God and began to pray, "Dear God, thank you for your guidance and support with my fishing. I have been able to provide for my family and for the village with the skills you have blessed upon me. Tonight I will be fishing again; please allow me to reap the benefits of your bounty and return safely to my family and village. Thank you, God."

BE **BAD**!

He stood, but before he could exit the church door, two police officers and the rich man barged in. The rich man then accused the fisherman of stealing his money, and the police officers took him into custody. Peter, who was watching all this happen, could not take it anymore. The injustice of what was happening was too much for him to bear. The fisherman was not the thief. The poor man was, and the rich man should get his money returned. He stepped out of the statue and explained exactly what had happened. The fisherman was released, the poor man was arrested, and the rich man was given his billfold of money. Peter felt happy that he was able to make things right.

Just then, God returned and asked how things went. Peter explained what had happened and what he had done in a proud way. God looked at him with great concern. He said, "I told you not to interfere." Peter said, "I know, but it was so clear and obvious what needed to be done. I knew what I was doing was right." God said, "You have made a disastrous mistake." "How could I have made a mistake? It was so clear what was happening," said Peter. God paused and explained what really happened. "The rich man I have blessed with all the abundance and riches in life, but he has been selfish and not giving of the abundance back to the community. Leaving his billfold was my way of giving back to the community. The poor man has done everything for his family and the community and for me. He deserved to be granted a blessing for service. The billfold of cash was for him to support his family. The fisherman, because you kept him out of jail tonight, will perish at sea in a severe storm. I wanted him to be arrested so as to protect him from the disastrous storm," God said.

Where in life do you insist you are doing the right thing? Just maybe there is another way of viewing the situation. It is time to have faith and to trust that what is happening is the right thing.

So Be Bold! Have faith that whatever is happening is happening for a greater reason than you can ever imagine.

APPLICATION: HAVE FAITH IN YOUR DESTINY

There are many practices to enhance the practice of faith. I am not an expert in this, yet many of my life situations have continued to enhance my practice of faith. Here are some ideas to open up and deepen the conversation of faith.

1. At a personal level

   a. A simple practice would be to ask yourself this question: What good will come from this situation? As we learned, we are not necessarily looking for an immediate answer to come from our brain, even though that is our nature. We are just sending the question out to the Universe to reveal a greater answer for us.

   Two of life's wisdom quotes come to mind here.

   ▸ *"Time will heal all wounds."* Be patient and allow the time necessary for the answers to appear.

   ▸ *"God's denial is not God's decline."* We sometimes wonder why things do not work out and figure they will never work out. Benjamin Franklin had many declines before he had one yes, and the world is a better place for it. Trust the greater path for your life.

   b. Quiet the mind practice

   There are many ways to allow a different perspective in when we quiet the mind. I will list a few for you to consider.

   ▸ **Connect into nature**—Deepak Chopra speaks to this point in his book, *The Seven Spiritual Laws of Success.* Try to connect into the abundance and flow that nature allows.

> ‣ Meditate—There are many forms of meditation. Chopra states, "In this space between our thoughts is where we can connect into a deeper level of awareness."
>
> ‣ Focusing activities—Get into the flow of things. I find that when we have focused practices, we can let go of the world and connect into a higher place. For me, fly fishing is an opening into this space.

2. At a spiritual level

   Begin connecting to a religious or spiritual practice. There are many groups available to freely explore. The key is to connect to a discourse which you feel connects you to a place where you feel the presence and power of a greater good.

BE BOLD: WRAP UP

On the journey to reclaiming your Badass self, it is critical to Be Bold. I have discussed new processes, practices, and thinking that will help you leverage your powerful biology and unique history; eliminate past stories that no longer serve you; engage the power of your mind to support your quest; use "Conversation for Action" to move with more rigor; build your Badass template as a tool to help you take Big stands in the world; and finally, have faith around who you are and the path you travel.

———

FOUR

BE BAD

"I'm Bad, I'm Nationwide." –ZZ *Top*

Thirty years ago, I was in a place of unashamed capacity; I felt I was unstoppable and invincible. I was 18 and a senior in high school. This was the year that I broke out of the walnut-strong shell I had built around myself for a half decade. In 1974, I moved to California from Oregon during my sixth-grade summer. This transition was difficult for me. I fell into a deep hole during the five years leading up to my senior year. I was in survival mode, and had lost some of my confidence about who I was as a young man from Oregon. I became a follower, standing on the sideline and staying far under the radar. Then my world significantly shifted. I suffered a serious knee injury in football during my junior year, and my parents told me I couldn't play football in my senior year. I was devastated. I loved football, and the field was one of the few places where I felt comfortable expressing myself with my biggest energy. I was rewarded for being Big, **Bold**, and **Bad** when I played football.

What happened to me that senior year was quite life transformational, and it set a new direction for me. I began to rediscover my SELF again after I had let it disappear for the past half-decade. My anger over not being able to play football mobilized me to change my behavior to earn the respect of my peers who were playing football. I began to take on other sports and excel in them to prove I was a great athlete, a great competitor, and a Badass. I started with skiing. I had never skied before, but everyone viewed it as the ultimate sport, and I decided I would become great at it. I skied roughly 30 days that winter, most days wearing my old football jersey, attacking the slope as if I was the linebacker of my past life. I sought out the most challenging runs and found every jump that allowed me to soar. When I look back, I realize it was my determination to prove myself as a man that led me to finding myself again. In order to ski every weekend, I had to hitch rides with anyone heading on the four-hour journey to Tahoe. This started to break down my stories about who I was, what was possible when I put my mind to it, and how there were many other great people in the world outside my clique. That year I also wrestled, ran the 440 track event, and lifted weights. My friendships expanded as I continued to stretch my limits and common sense about who I was and who I could be.

The song, "I'm Bad, I'm Nationwide," was released in November 1979— the beginning of my senior year and in the middle of football season.

The phrase "I'm bad. I'm nationwide," became my battle cry. It became the affirmation that kept me on track as I rediscovered my true self. Fast forward more than 30 years, and the battle cry is back. I have been on a similar quest over the past decade to rediscover myself. In 2008, the same injured knee became damaged to the point that I needed reconstructive surgery. My world again shifted in unexpected ways. I left a corporate role at Motorola to start my own coaching company; my marriage of 22 years ended; I experienced extremely challenging issues relating to my children, which I never dreamt would happen to my kids; and I became lost on who I was. All I built and counted on was gone, and I did not know this new man. Then without any warning, I lost both my parents.

As I write this book about becoming Big, Bold, and Bad again, I know it is my calling. I was called to step into all of my life's work and experiences, and show up as a Badass in spite of all the life challenges I have encountered. Like in 1979, I now have to step up to a place beyond myself and push myself to Be Big, Bold, and Bad, and to do whatever it takes to survive, thrive, and show up in my unstoppable power to help others in life.

In this section, I want to take what we have learned in the Be Big and Be Bold sections and begin to leverage it to become your own definition of Badass. I say this because sometimes we associate the word Bad or Badass with a negative space, but that is not how I define it here. Urban Dictionary defines Badass as "Ultra Cool." I believe being a Badass in life is showing up in your Biggest expression of yourself, boldly living your unique and powerful life, and being Bad (meaning good) by going after your dreams and life's calling. Badass is also a word that can bring some powerful emotion to the table. To test this out, say the following line aloud, "I am a Badass." What do you feel after you say that a few times? Do you feel more alive? Do you feel confident and brave? To be clear, being a Badass

> ...BEING BAD, I LOOK AT HOW WE LIVE OUR PURPOSE, IGNITE OUR PASSION, AND BRING OUT THAT UNSTOPPABLE POWER

does not mean being an asshole or criminal or give you permission in any way to hurt or harm anyone. It is an exciting feeling knowing you are playing at the top of your game in career, relationships, and life. So now is your time to step up to **Be Bad**!

When I consider being Bad, I look at how we live our purpose, ignite our passion, and bring out that unstoppable power. After doing the earlier exercises, you have created a great view of who you are and a template to where you show up in your Biggest and best. You have learned how to quiet your internal conversations and restrictions that limit your thinking and action. So how do you want to show up now in the world? What are you called to do? The beautiful thing about bringing attention to who you are is that attention brings awareness, awareness brings focus, focus brings energy, and that is where things happen. All changes happen when we get the emotional energy engaged.

Simon Sinek has a great TED Talk that explores the power of WHY.

He speaks about how people buy products based on emotions and not on the facts. If you want to step into your Badness, it is critical to get that same emotional engagement. Your good ideas are the first step. You also need to create that exciting energy that keeps you up at night with a zest for life. Becoming a Badass is outside the realm of what is normal. It is time to follow the dream. Famous sales trainer Zig Ziglar said, "What you can conceive and believe, you can achieve." This statement is told in many different ways by many different authors and leaders. Funny thing is you hear it so much that it almost has lost its punch, yet it is one of the most powerful statements about making new things in the world possible. Steve Jobs was the rock star example of this. He would dream up ideas and believe in them to the point where everyone else believed, and well, the world is a different place because of this type of belief. Can you take this statement to heart? History is littered with example after example of how "what was not possible" was made possible by dreamers believing it will happen and then making it happen.

Therefore, your challenge is to take on this task to conceive your dream, believe it will happen, and then go out and get it done. We have done the prep-work. Your Badass is waiting. Your Badass is uniquely you because it is what you have been designed to do. TIME TO STEP UP!

 MOOD CHECK
Becoming aware of your moods at this stage will help you choose how you want to see the world, as well as help you discover your progress and the changes taking place in you.

1. What is your mood now?

2. Did anything with this work or outside this work trigger you into your current mood?

3. Is that the optimum mood for this work?

4. Can you change it to a more powerful mood? How?

BE BAD—STEP ONE

Step one is to dream and conceive what you really want to accomplish now that you have your foundation piece in place. I would like you to refresh yourself with all your answers from the previous sections, revealing your unique insights, gifts and power that no one in the world has in their entirety like you.

Be Bad is really all about bringing your biggest energy to the table. It is like you have built the rocket, and now you need the fuel to launch it. Similar to a rocket breaking through the atmosphere, the initial amount of fuel and energy required is impressive, but once you get through the initial hurdle, the ball is rolling, and the energy required to keep it going into the land of your dreams does not need much effort. Yet, most people say, "This does not feel right" or "But that is not who I am." Our old restrictive shapes and stories are so powerful—like that of gravity on Earth—that you have to step up to a much higher level of excitement, energy, and commitment to make it happen. Can you make the commitment to step up?

YOU MUST HAVE A 100% COMMITMENT TO THE CHANGE.

Many teachers in the world promote this simple mindset, but most people cannot truly understand the significance. Many people do not know why this mindset is critical to succeed in the change they desire. This commitment is best described by a story called "Burn the Boats." In the story an island tribe battles the neighboring island tribe, and the warriors travel via boats to reach the other island. As they all came ashore, one warrior looked back to see all the boats were on fire. He quickly asked the chief of the warriors what was happening. The chief responded, "There is no turning back, we either win the battle or die."

The boats represent the easy way out if things do not quite work out. The metaphors of the boats in our life are many, and they provide us with reasons not to completely commit to the new outcome. By burning the boats, there is no option of turning back to the way things were. As we discussed, what you conceive and believe, you can achieve. You would not be on this new island as a warrior ready to fight if this was not critical to you. The old way no longer serves you for your travels to this new destination. So why leave a lifeboat in place? Life is about growth and moving forward in your journey. If we stand still or go backwards, what is really happening? We are settling! There is no progress in settling. Without progress, we regress.

This is not your first voyage to reclaim your Big, Bold, and Bad Island. You have been there before, but the 100 percent commitment was missing, and you did not "burn the boats." So when it got messy, well, you just turned around and went back home. Another powerful story, "The Cup and the Quart," illustrates the difficulty of letting go of the old to go after the new. Imagine you are holding a cup in your hand. The cup represents your current life. It is nice and comfortable to hold onto this cup of life, and yet you feel or know that there is more to life than just the cup you currently hold. Then because you have opened your mind up to the possibility of more, the brain seeks out the answer, as we learned in the Be Bold section. What appears is something new, bigger, and better— the quart, or four cups of life. Here is where the challenge exists. In order to get to the quart, you have to set down the cup and begin the process of reaching to grab the quart. This

"BE BAD" IS REALLY ALL ABOUT BRINGING YOUR BIGGEST ENERGY TO THE TABLE

is where people panic, lose focus, and begin to question if this will happen. When you set down the cup and reach for the quart, you are holding nothing in your hands. You have nothing, and without the "burn the boats" type of commitment, the cup looks better than nothing. This will make you lose interest in going further. How many times has this happened to me? Quite a few, but I have also experienced the 100 percent commitment with great success.

So why does the "burn the boats" strategy work? Well, it aligns all your Badass energy toward the change. Your focus is clear, your stories are empowering, and your body is mobilized to win. Think about times in the past when you have deployed the "burn the boats" strategy. Did you accomplish the goal or discover something even better on the other side? The rewards are great for those who travel this path. If you do not believe me, chat with the people who are in their Badass, and see how they got there. You might be surprised to hear the pattern show up repeatedly.

Therefore, it is time to burn the boats, break the cup, and begin the journey to your ultimate Badass life and lifestyle.

BUILD YOUR 100 PERCENT COMMITMENT TO THE BAD YOU!

What will it cost you to be 100 percent committed to becoming the Badass you are? Here are two steps to build that commitment. Let us first look at why it is tough to move away from the cup to the quart. We are biologically designed to unconsciously look at every situation as a survival situation. A portion of our brain determines the road we must choose in a life-threatening situation. Our body mobilizes to take action around this survival instinct. These instincts are rooted around pleasure and pain. We will move toward pleasure and away from pain, but the movement away from pain seems to be the primary motivator of the pair. Pain and pleasure are interpretations. Therefore, we may think something will be painful and avoid it, but if we re-examine it from a new perspective, it may be quite pleasurable. In addition, the levels of pain we can tolerate are very important variables to consider. Some people have more life experience and can tolerate what some believe as overwhelming pain, and others have built an emotional and physical threshold to find the power or the pleasure of the event instead of being consumed by it.

So why is this relevant to us in building our Badass self? I want to deploy both pain and pleasure to ground you in your 100 percent commitment to your Badass self. I want to use perception of pain to reveal how the rest of your life will turn out if you do not commit to your Badass self today. I want to create a feeling that if you do not change, life would be more of the same—a place where you never reached your dream, a place where you played small and did not contribute your gifts.

BE BAD: THE PAIN OF STAYING THE SAME

In this exercise it is important to shift your old patterns. This will require some very Big energy. Some of our patterns have been locked in with us for our entire lifetime. Like extracting gold ore embedded in quartz, this requires some sort of tremendous force. To get to the 100 percent focus and commitment to change is no different. In this exercise I am going to ask you to stir your emotions, get angry, and take yourself to a dark place where life does not work out and where your Badass story is just a faint memory. *(Disclaimer: This exercise is not intended to take you to a place that is not recoverable. It is a first pass at opening you up to why the "cup" lifestyle is no longer a strategy that will serve you as you go forward. It is an exercise where you begin to see why "burning the boats" is critical for the success of reclaiming your Badass.)*

 EXERCISE: THE PAIN IF WE DON'T CHANGE

1. Find a place (room) where you can fully express yourself. This should be a private place where the entirety of the experience can express itself. An option: have a friend or spouse walk you through the exercise, supporting you with the questions and holding the space for you while you go deep.

2. Sit down, close your eyes, and begin a deep breathing practice. This will begin to settle the body and mind into the moment.

3. Speak the following affirmations to set the intention of the exercise:

   a. *I will open fully to explore the consequences of my life if I do not change.*

   b. *I will allow myself to fully experience the emotions associated with not changing.*

4. Now tell yourself the current challenges you are experiencing in your life. This is not a time to hold back. You are at this stage of the book, and you are here for a reason. Start to express your dissatisfaction with your job, career, life, and relationships. It is good to vent. Allow the emotions to stir up the energy in your body. The more energy you bring to your language, the more you will begin to feel the consequences of where you are today.

   (Please note: This exercise is about creating a story of how the future will turn out if you do not change today. The more courageous you are in allowing yourself to feel the negative space that will be your future if you do not change, will make the difference in how you proceed forward. We are creating pain that will mobilize your survival instinct to seek out a new way to create an incredible life.)

6. Keeping your eyes closed, take a few deep breaths to re-center yourself into your intention, and say to yourself:

   a . *I will openly explore the consequences of my life in 10 years if I do not change.*

   b. *I will allow myself to fully experience the emotions associated with not changing.*

7. Now, visualize 10 years from today. Place yourself in that moment by speaking your age and seeing your life and relationships as if you are there.

8. Tell yourself the challenges you are experiencing in your life 10 years from now. This is not a time to hold back. Start to express your anticipated dissatisfaction with your job, career, life, and relationships.

9. Now go to the end of your life. Place yourself in that moment by speaking your age and seeing your life and relationships as if you were there.

10. Speak to yourself of the current challenges you are experiencing at the end of your life. This is not a time to hold back. Start to express your anticipated dissatisfaction with your career, life, and relationships.

You may even want to consider using this last reflection of the end of your life as a chance to write your own eulogy as if you did not change or step up into your Biggest, Boldest and Baddest self. This eulogy about a person who did not become a Badass, but instead just settled, will be shared with all your loved ones, family, friends, peers, and community. Can you imagine what they are saying about how you had so much potential, yet it was wasted or, worse yet, how you failed them? This is the type of pain you have to experience to mobilize you today so that will not happen tomorrow. Build this pain to fully see that you have to commit 100% to this change. Use this painful vision to ignite the fire and burn the boats.

APPLICATION: PAIN OF STAYING THE SAME

Now that you have allowed yourself to fully experience the consequences of not taking action today, I would like you to write down those feelings and emotions in your journal.

1. Capture the pain associated with not taking action today.

2. What were the feelings associated with not shifting your trajectory?

3. Write down how it affects your life, relationships, family, and career.

4. Have you generated enough energy to say, "I am mad as Hell, and I am not going to take this anymore"?

This document will help you stay focused when you want to go back to the "cup." This is the "burn the boats" document. There is no option to go back, and nothing worth retreating to.

BE BAD: THE PLEASURE OF STEPPING INTO YOUR BADASS

Now let us create the pleasure of what happens in your life when you make the change and become your Badass again. This will help pull you forward during those times of question. It is critical to allow your creativity to flourish. Do not screen your thoughts to make this small or question if it is even possible. That is not the purpose. It is to let go and experience your full expression of who you can be when you fully claim your Badass again!

EXERCISE: THE PLEASURE OF STEPPING INTO YOUR BADASS

1. Find a place where you can fully express yourself. This place should be a private place where you can feel the entirety of this experience. An option: have a friend or spouse walk you through the exercise, supporting you

with the questions and holding the space for you while you go deep.

2. Sit down, close your eyes, and begin a deep breathing practice. This will begin to settle the body and mind into the moment.

3. Speak the following affirmations to set the intention of the exercise.

   a. *I will openly explore the positive outcomes of my life when I step back into my Badass.*

   b. *I will allow myself to fully experience the emotions associated with becoming my Badass again.*

4. Now tell yourself the current excitement you feel about making the change. What does it mean to you? This is not a time to hold back. You are at the stage of the book where you have built the foundation to regain your Badass. Start to fully express your satisfaction with how things will be in your job, career, life, and relationships if you begin the change. It is critical to get excited here. Allow the emotions to stir up the energy and feelings in your body. The more energy you bring to your language, the more you will begin to truly feel the excitement about what happens with your change.

   (Please note: This exercise is about creating a story of how the future will turn out with your new commitment to becoming your Badass again. The more open you are to exploring the future, and the feelings and emotions associated with it, the more the body will desire the pleasure.)

5. Continue with your eyes closed and take a few more

cleansing deep breaths. This will encourage the body and mind to stay present for the exercise.

6. Take yourself forward to 10 years from now and experience the excitement of where you are now because you made the change. What does it mean to you? This is not a time to hold back.

7. Start to fully envision and express how things will be in your job, career, life, and relationships if you are a Badass.

8. Continue with your eyes closed and take a few more cleansing deep breaths. This will encourage the body and mind to stay present for the exercise.

9. Take yourself to the end of your life, and experience the excitement of where you are now because you made the change. What does it mean to you? This is not a time to hold back. Start to fully envision and express how things are in your life, career, and relationships as you live in your fullness!

10. You may even want to consider using this last reflection of the end of your life as a chance to write your own eulogy, as if you changed and stepped up into your Biggest, Boldest and Baddest self. This eulogy is about a person who did become a Badass. What would you like to share with all your loved ones, family, friends, peers, and community? Can you imagine what they are saying about you? How they would express with joy how you fully experienced the love, success, and wealth of living a life in all your potential and power! This is the type of pleasure you have to experience to mobilize you today so you can make this happen tomorrow.

APPLICATION: THE PLEASURE OF STEPPING INTO YOUR BADASS
Now that you have fully allowed yourself to experience the greatness by taking action today, I would like you to write down your feelings and emotions in your journal.

1. Capture the pleasure that you have associated with taking action today.

2. What were the feelings associated with shifting your trajectory?
   a. How will it affect your life, relationships, and career?
   b. Do you feel that you generated enough energy to say, "Yes!" to make it happen?

These two exercises should provide the pleasure and the pain needed to help commit to reclaiming your Big, Bold, and Bad Self. I have had a chance to go through this exercise in a number of different ways over the years, yet Tony Robbins does a magnificent job of walking people through the pain and pleasure exercise at his Unleash the Power Within (UPW) events. I would recommend attending one of his big events if you would like to continue to enhance your awareness and motivation around using this technique.

BE BAD: BUILD YOUR VISION FOR A BADASS LIFE

By now you should have built the 100% commitment level using your new stories around the pleasure of changing and the pain of staying the same. Next let's take the exercise you just accomplished and use it to create your Badass vision going forward. The following reflection exercise will begin to build more contexts for your Badass vision. For this exercise, set yourself up with 30 minutes to reflect on these questions in a stream-of-thought writing session without censoring, editing, or spell checking. Your quick, top-of-mind responses are best. Trust that whatever comes out will be a valuable guidepost for taking action.

EXERCISE: EXPLORE YOUR VISION

1. Ask yourself these questions:
   a. If you had unlimited resources at your disposal, what dreams do you want to accomplish?
   b. What is your life purpose here on this planet?
   c. Why is that important to you?
   d. How would you be applying your Big and Bold energy for maximum impact in your life?
   e. If you were told that you have a short time to live, would you have any regrets about things you had not accomplished?
   f. What do you do so well that it does not feel like work and that makes you happy?
   g. What do you love to do?

2. Review Your Answers
   a. How do they make you feel?
   b. What new thinking opened up for you after reviewing all your answers?
   c. What have you allowed to sit on the sideline for far too long?
   d. Where are the emotions surfacing around your answers?
   e. Where are you upset with yourself for not getting these things done?
   f. What is calling to you to show up and go after it with all your Big, Bold, and Bad power?

APPLICATION—CREATE YOUR VISION

1. Create your vision: Use the theme of I am a Badass; I know who I am and how to Be Big; I know how to Be Bold and to fend off the limiting thinking that holds me back. Now write the vision for how this is going to manifest in your life. What are you going to do with your life as you go forward? What are you called to do? Write down in your journal your dream as a Badass. Feel the excitement of this unlimited thinking. Let it flow. This is your Badass manifesto.

   ‣ My vision is: "I am called to lead others to their unique power and freedom." I want to reach millions of people through my Big, Bold, and Badass efforts. I will play on a global scale, influencing people to live the life of their dreams, and fully embrace and enjoy the journey of full expression and power.

2. Now take your vision and test it. Practice saying it many times. Does it excite you? Can you begin to feel the power of the impact it has on you, others, and the world? This is critical to get you to an emotional level that begins to shift your entire being. In this practice of saying it aloud, the body begins the process of reshaping. The more energy you bring to yourself when saying your vision, the deeper the impact it will have on you. I suggest that you say this many times a day for a week.

   ‣ You are training your mind to own your vision of your Badass, and conditioning your mind to seek the resources to fulfill that vision.

BE BAD: USE YOUR BODY TO SUPPORT YOUR NEW BADASS VISION

We have just built a 100% commitment to changing and have created our Badass vision. Now we need to align the body to support us. As we previously discussed, we are our practices.

What we do every day shapes who we are. Shifting our focus to become a Badass requires new practices to reshape from our old ways to the new ones required to hold our vision.

THE MORE ENERGY YOU BRING TO YOURSELF WHEN SAYING YOUR VISION, THE DEEPER THE IMPACT IT WILL HAVE ON YOU.

Whenever we take on a new role, we have to shift our practices.

For example when you become an executive, you have to take on new leadership practices; to become an auto mechanic, new physical practices are required, too. There are practices for everything that shift and shape the body. If you have ever declared that you wish to accomplish a certain physical activity or goal, then the process requires you to work at the practice until the body reshapes to support the new action. Think about what happens in our body when we take on a new sport.

Around 20 years ago, I declared I wanted to become a mountain bike rider. This activity was important to me for many reasons, so I began the new practice. WOW, my body was in no way set up to handle my new goal or vision! At the time, bikes were not designed to offer much comfort to the rider; for months, if not years, my body had to shape and reshape to accommodate the demands of riding a mountain bike on the trails. My body began to shape around the new level of endurance and breathing patterns. My body started strengthening the muscles to handle the unique mechanics of the bike, getting used to a sore rear end all the time, cramps in the forearms from gripping the brakes, and painful kidney shakes from the constant bouncing as I raced downhill. My body was taxed to the point of throwing up, hitting the wall when I had no energy left to ride one more foot. Then there were challenges with clipping in and out of the toe clips and, of course, the occasional fall. As you can see, for me to transition from the "cup" of riding a bike recreationally with the kids to the "quart" of scaling mountains required new practices focused on the body, which eventually reshaped my body to the bike and experience of mountain bike riding.

Consider the fundamental truth, "You are your practices; change your practices, change your life." What new physical practices do you need to put in place to help you become the Badass you outlined above in your vision? For me, my old practices created shapes that had taken hold for decades. To Be Bad, I had to take on new practices to support my vision.

The practice you declare to support the development of the Badass can be anything. It is important to find activities that, with the right engagement, will bring the necessary energy and body awareness you need to transcend the old shape. We need to commit to practices that expand us out of the box. Here is the opportunity to reinforce this Bad state with your Badass vision.

I have engaged in high-energy practices that resulted in a massive change of my biology, such as kickboxing, hitting a heavy bag, and sprinting uphill. I have also engaged in other practices such as Tai Chi, Qi Gong, Aikido, meditation, and Bikram yoga to shift my old patterns and develop a new leadership presence. For example, I used Bikram yoga to support me on my Be Bad vision. Bikram yoga is a practice of doing 26 yoga positions in 105-degree heat. As a beginner, I was concerned about the intensity of the activity, but I built the story of how it would help with my health, posture, presence, and emotional strength. I discovered that the intensity of the movements and the heat caused me to build a new awareness of my focus, breath, and endurance. I began practicing three times a week, and my energy continued to increase and grow. I began to shift my physical shape, my knowledge of what I was capable of enduring, and my focus—all critical aspects of me being my Bad.

BUILD THE "BE BAD" BODY

Pump yourself up! I have coached executives, high production sales professionals, and people in life transitions. One commonality I have found with people at the top of their game is that they perform daily practices that PUMP THEM UP. Generating energy for the day ahead or for an important meeting where you are going to show up in your Badass requires a "Get Pumped" action to charge the system.

Each of us has done these routines occasionally, but they can mean the difference between whether your Badass or the dumbed-down version of you shows up. At a workshop I was leading, I brought forth this concept, and I asked the participants—who were the top 10 percent income earners focused on increasing their sales production for their sales organization—to demonstrate how they pumped themselves up prior to a big sales meeting. These salespeople earned between $300,000 and $1 million a year in commissions. I knew to achieve this level of production, the ability to bring their Big, Bold, and Bad to the table every time was critical. A man stood up and said, "I will demonstrate." He was one of the inspirational leaders of this high production group with a personality that everyone liked. I asked him to show us, and to everyone's surprise, he let go with a huge display of energy, pumping his arms back and forth, building the charge in his body. Imagine a light version of the Warner Bros. Tasmanian Devil cartoon character! As he continued, we saw his energy rise to a powerful level. When he finished, he said he does this every day and prior to meetings.

EXERCISE: PUMP YOURSELF UP!

What energy routine can you create for yourself that you can practice daily to pump yourself up? Examples:

> ▸ Take few deep breaths, with loud full body inhales/exhales.

> ▸ Practice loud positive self-talk in the car to amplify your energy level.

> ‣ Create your own version of the Tasmanian Devil cartoon character. Move your body in a big way to break away the cobwebs of life and release your natural energy.

SHOW UP BIG IN YOUR FRAME

Amy Cuddy presented some very interesting findings in a very popular TED Talk entitled, *"Your Body Language Shapes Who You Are."* She reported that by taking a power stance with either of our hands on our hips, or our arms open in a victory stance, we create a physiology shift in the body that makes us feel stronger, or like a Badass. She suggests holding this pose for two minutes a day, as well as just before important meetings.

At a speaker-training event, the teacher spoke about how important it is for speakers to own their space. Your space is the area that surrounds your body as wide as your arms can stretch from side to side, top to bottom, and front to back. She indicated that when we look at someone, we are subconsciously checking to see if the speaker fills up his or her space. Do they own it? If not, we question why the speaker is playing small or wonder what he or she might be hiding.

EXERCISE: USING NEW PRACTICES TO BUILD YOUR BADASS

1. **Power Stance:** Begin a daily practice of Be Bad with your body by holding your power stance for two minutes. Track your progress.

2. **Own Your Space:** When you speak, walk, and take action, open up your movements to take up more space. Speak with bigger arm and hand gestures. Fill up the personal space and Be Bad.

3. **Stand Up:** A simple exercise is to stand up whenever you speak. It will not only mobilize and increase your

energy, but it will do the same to everyone else. Bringing fresh energy to a meeting can only enhance the environment.

 EXERCISE: THE POWER OF YOUR HANDSHAKE

There are many ways to use the power of your body to embrace the Be Bad presence you want to cultivate. You are training your body with new practices to shift the shape and be able to execute, instead of succumbing to old powerful patterns that want to keep you small. You are introducing what appear to be simple practices to build your awareness of how subtle changes can start the momentum. Success breeds success, and when you begin any new practice, it should be easy to win. This will keep you on track as the body begins to reshape to the place where you are a Badass again. The handshake exercise allows you to show up in a very powerful way that aligns with an acceptable practice in most Western cultures.

Touch is a powerful way to break barriers. The handshake is a powerful tool. The process of centered handshakes:

1. Clear your mind and leave the bags at the door.
2. Quickly go through leadership presence alignment.
3. Extend your energy, assess, and feel the person's presence.
4. Begin the handshake, and then settle into the handshake. Feel the connection.
5. Say "Hello!"
6. Am I present; are they there; can I connect in a deep and meaningful way?

7. Release the handshake, yet stay present to the situation.

8. Smile!

APPLICATION—BRIDGE THE GAP

1. Get clear on the gap which exists between where you are today and the Badass you will become. This assessment can come from you and from others. Please note: No matter how big the gap, with the right practices and intentions, you will be able to bridge it.

2. Declare new practices to bridge the gap.

a. Based on your vision, start stepping up the specific training around building the embodied skills to support being Bad. It is important to be in action when reshaping the body. It has to move and experience the new behavior to begin the transformation to Being Bad.

b. 60 days Big energy practice—Take on an activity that pushes you beyond your normal physical practice, such as Bikram yoga, kickboxing, or a 400-meter race; or commit to a physical challenge such as the Spartan, Tough Mudder, Death Ride, or whatever calls to you. The goal is that the activity push the limits (mind and body) of what you think you can do. Take on a project that forces you to be in your Bad. Make a commitment to others to take on a project that allows you to push yourself in this new area. The beauty of this is that the experience will reshape you by requiring you to step up. For example, I committed to apearing in several TV and radio interviews that forced me to be Big, Bold, and Bad.

BE BAD: GUIDANCE FROM THE HEAVENS ABOVE!

In this Be Bad section and throughout this book, I have talked about reclaiming your Badass from three perspectives: Mind, Body, and Spirit. I am going to venture to say that most of us live our life primarily from the perspective of the Mind. We exert little or no focus on the Body as a tool of intelligence and extraordinary power as we design and act in our lives, and we do not focus on the power of the Spirit. The power of "Spirit," "God," or the "Universe" is a conversation that can be viewed as taboo. But I am going to say that when pressed about the existence of something greater than us, most of us would say that there is a greater force. However, even with this acknowledgement, our practices to tap into and align with a higher power are rare. Please forgive me if your spiritual practices are rock solid, but what I have found is that most people don't call God or the Universe into their daily life unless there is a very serious situation.

I saw a perfect illustration of how, when life is on the line, God becomes real, and God's support is repeatedly sought. The year was 2012, and the brave Nik Wallenda was going to walk a tightrope across the Grand Canyon. Check it out on YouTube in the video entitled, "Nik Wallenda Crosses 1,500 Foot Grand Canyon Gorge on Tightrope." They interviewed him before the walk, and all seemed okay. Then, he climbed the wire secured several feet from the edge of the canyon and began the walk toward the rim. As his walk led him over the edge of the canyon, he began to speak to God with a frequency that I had never seen before on national TV. I do not know his religious practices or affiliations, but it was clear that in this step-by-step life or death situation, he switched his orientation toward God for guidance and support. He was asking genuinely for God's support on this journey. Have you asked God or the Universe to support you in a life or death situation? Or a situation you felt was out of your control? I would venture to say yes. Could you imagine if you could have the faith to call on God or the Universe for your everyday actions, instead of waiting for those life or death moments?

I have always paid attention to the spiritual side of my life, but I had not developed a relationship with God until about five years ago as I began to re-examine my life. As I have moved into a closer relationship with God, I find two lessons stand out for me.

‣ There are situations beyond my understanding, and I can go deep and dark trying to make sense of it all, yet I have found that I am most peaceful when I let go. I say to myself, "This is beyond me, and I have faith that what will happen will be right for me and others." There is a bigger story happening that I cannot even imagine, and I trust whatever happens is supposed to happen.

‣ We are on a path to show up in our Biggest and serve our family, the community, and ourselves. Some of us are called early to begin this journey, and some of us are gifted with life lessons to prepare us for when we are called to serve. We will know when it is time to serve, how to be courageous to begin this journey, and how to do what it takes to get to our fullest potential.

BE BAD: WHAT ARE YOU CALLED TO DO?

Be Bad is about tapping into your Bigger purpose. In 2004, I discovered that coaching was a profession that called me to serve. I left Palm Inc. to pursue this passion and begin the process of becoming a somatic coach. I chose somatic coaching because of its emphasis on helping others through transition and focusing on the wholeness of the body with a deep emphasis on working through the body. I found that this style of coaching discourse helped me move quickly through life situations, and it felt natural to work with people at this level.

In late 2004, an event occurred that aligned me with my purpose on this planet and reinforced how I can serve others in an extraordinary way. It was the last day of a five-day intensive training course for my somatic coaching credential. The instructor pulled me aside and informed me that my brother was on the phone, and I should go take the call. I spoke to my brother and found out that our mother was in a life-threatening situation. She had been through stomach surgery two weeks prior, and all seemed to be good, but now she was back in the hospital, and her outlook was not promising. I immediately dismissed myself from the course and began the two-and-a-half-hour journey to the hospital.

As I drove, I began to pray to God for her recovery. I also suspected I might play a role in her recovery. I was trained to help people tap into the power of their own body to self-heal, self-generate, and self-educate. I began to realize that I could save my mom's life, and I started to talk myself into bringing the Biggest energy and my education to the hospital to help my mom. I arrived at my mom's hospital room and entered to find a very chaotic situation. My dad was arguing with the doctor to do something, and the doctor was stating that they could not figure out what was wrong with her. All tests showed that she should be okay. In the background I heard the faint moans of my mother.

IMAGINE IF YOU COULD HAVE THE FAITH TO CALL ON GOD OR THE UNIVERSE FOR YOUR EVERYDAY ACTIONS, INSTEAD OF WAITING FOR THOSE LIFE OR DEATH MOMENTS?

I normally would move right in and take charge; but this time, I stood back and observed the situation. I began centering myself to be as present and open as possible for what was to come. The argument abruptly ended, and my dad and the doctor left the room in frustration. I decided it was time to see my mom. When I pulled back the curtain, what I saw was not good. Imagine seeing your mom in a state where it felt like you were looking at a dying person. Her skin was pale, her face was hollow, her eyes were scared, and her voice was weak. I regained my balance after the initial shock, approached my mother, and grasped her hand. Her grip was weak, her touch was cold, and her energy was trembling. I knew immediately this was my time to step up and have the faith that I was there for a reason, and my training was needed.

I began talking with her to assess the situation. I began to use my somatic training to look at three key areas: her language, her focus, and, finally, her life force. I remembered the doctor saying that they had done all the tests, and nothing should be wrong.

In my conversation with my mom, I began to see the dark space my mother had created in her mind. It was a place so dark that she assumed she was dying, and that intense emotional focus was mobilizing her entire being to believe it. She spoke about not wanting to eat because she was afraid that eating would intensify the pain and quicken the death process. She was convinced she was dying, and her life force was already vacating her body. She was unconsciously abandoning her basic mechanics of bringing life energy into the body. Her breath was shallow and deprived her body of this precious energy. She was giving up. She had allowed her focus, language, and body to work against her instead of for her. This is where I decided I had the capacity to make a difference. I was not going to let my mother continue down this path of self-destruction. I centered myself and became as present with her as possible. I tightened my grip on her hand, and I looked deeply into her eyes. She is the woman who gave me the gift of life. It was now my turn to return that gift. I took a deep breath, and in a caring, but steadfast voice told her, "You are not dying. I am going to work with you and bring the life force back. You are going to feel better soon." I smiled with confidence and love, and began the process. The first step was to change her language, so I offered different interpretations about pain. I continued to shift her language as we talked more about the operation's success and what the doctors had told dad about all the test results being positive. In our conversations I kept changing her focus from death to life. Pain was now associated with recovery and not death. Next, I began the somatic energy work to summon her body's own internal healing powers. I asked her to bring deep breaths into the stomach area to allow the contraction of her pain to shift, allowing her body and muscles to relax away from death's grip on her. I added a focused touch to her stomach to greater enhance her body's attention to the area. Wherever you put attention, energy will follow, and this energy was her own healing power. I continued to encourage different breathing patterns and also continued the somatic energy work on other areas of her body.

Within 10 minutes, she had completely changed. Her skin was flush, her face was full and alive, and her eyes engaging and optimistic. I decided to shift the story she had around putting food in her belly. She had imagined her stomach would explode, and she had stopped eating out of fear. Like with breath, food is a life energy that would restore her reserves, increase her energy, and help her gain more strength to support the recovery process. I shifted this story of "food meant death" to "food meant life," and I encouraged her to take a bite of the food sitting on the table next to her bed. She was willing to allow me to lead because of her love and trust for her son. Being centered and completely present, I fed her the first bit of food. It went down fine. She was hungry, and now that the first bit of food had opened the door, she wanted to eat more. Very quickly she was restoring more of her energy. I continued to reinforce her new focus, her new language, and her body's healing power. Just then, the nurse and doctor entered the room to check on my mom. I will never forget their expressions of complete shock and surprise. They both said, "What happened?" Mom had completely turned herself around to the point where she was ready to get up and leave, and they did not know what to say. It was such a complete turnaround. The nurse said it was a miracle, but my mom and I knew it was something different. Mom went home that afternoon and had no future problems with her stomach.

I realized that I am called to this work for a reason that extended beyond my mother. I am called to lead others to their unique power and freedom. Where have been those moments in your life where you knew you were called by a higher power to do what you do best? It is time to heed to your calling?

BE BAD: WRAP UP

What are you called to do? My life experience and work with others has revealed that there is a great calling for each of us on this planet. My hope is that in this Be Bad section, I have opened you up to the possibility that you can accomplish the life of your dreams and live your purpose. You took a trip into the future to reveal the pain of not stepping up to your calling and also saw the pleasure of fully embracing all that you were meant to be. With this commitment I asked you to create a Vision of greatness for you. And to ensure your success, we talked about supporting your journey with empowering practices which will build the new body and presence to achieve your goal. Finally, we talked about aligning with a greater force than yourself to help mobilize and support you in ways we cannot even imagine. Our quest of this Be Bad section is to bring together your Big and Bold insights from previous sections and align them around the Biggest, Boldest and Baddest expression of yourself possible... your Badass!

———————

FIVE

STAYING ON TRACK

How do you stay on track? We have now learned how your old patterns, habits, and beliefs can shape your every action. We have looked at processes and systems to bring awareness to what is stopping you, and we have opened up the options to choose how you would like to act. Once we make the choice, we have to create the energy internally to manifest this new change. Finally, we need to take the action to begin the process. I say "process" because, as I have discussed, habits live in the body and brain as automatic behaviors, hardened over decades of life. The only thing that will trump this deep pattern is 100 percent commitment to the new path and change you've designed.

In today's world, almost everything is changing so rapidly that relying on old patterns and insights will not get you far, and will most likely get you in trouble. The brain recalls these patterns and sets your body up for the appropriate action. Have you ever been in a conversation while you find yourself sitting with your arms folded? This reaction can be caused by a shift in the environment or to something someone said, and unconsciously you closed down to protect yourself. Our bodies have taken on many other habitual patterns and shapes around how we talk, walk, connect, engage with others, complete a task, eat and drink—anything and everything. Therefore, to make a change, you have to realize that the body is not a light switch which can be turned on to make everything right instantly. The body requires a big commitment to the change, a new pattern to adopt, and practice over time to build the behavior. You have to experience the breakdown repeatedly before the old pattern breaks down enough to create space for the new pattern to take shape.

> YOU HAVE TO EXPERIENCE THE BREAKDOWN REPEATEDLY BEFORE THE OLD PATTERN BREAKS DOWN ENOUGH TO CREATE SPACE FOR THE NEW PATTERN TO TAKE SHAPE

So how do you ensure the new (Big, Bold, and Bad) does not turn back into the old pattern? What support tools and resources can you enlist around yourself to give you the best chances of success in the long haul? I will list a couple of ideas in this section to keep you on track.

SIX STEPS TO SUCCEED THROUGH CHANGES AND TRANSITIONS

This is a process I discovered when I was attending an Al-Anon meeting. A wise man who has supported thousands of people and families along this difficult path shared this insight. He said that once you get the new practices of health and balance in place at a clinic, then most people leave and try to go it alone. Here the success factor drops tremendously. He said that even with support groups like Alcoholics Anonymous, with their regular meetings, many people fail and eventually fall right back into their old behavior. If they would follow these six steps, it would give them an 85 percent chance of success.

Over the years, I have seen how this powerful process can be applied to every change we make in life. It is a proven method to give you that extra advantage to truly step away from your old patterns and into your new Big, Bold, and Bad life.

Can you picture a situation in which a change that seemed so imperative, so important, and so critical did not happen for some reason? There are probably many reasons we can come up with to justify why the change did not happen, and, believe me, I know they all make sense. This is why change is so difficult. Our habits, patterns, and common sense will not allow the change to mess with our homeostasis. Our body's biology is designed to maintain at all costs our certainty that "all is okay," but our job now is to recognize a need for a change. We need to listen to the subtle whispers coming from within us that warn us "all is not okay." In order to break the bondage of these heavy chains, we have to evoke this powerful process to support ourselves with the resources required to ensure that we change. Let us explore the Six Steps to Success for Change.

SIX STEPS TO SUCCESS FOR CHANGE

1. You must have a 100 percent commitment to the change.
   a. This is a commitment you will not back off, no matter what.
   b. Your focus is strong, for example: "I will die if I don't change" or "This is killing me." This is a figurative statement, yet I hear people speak this way when they know it is time to change.
   c. "Burn the Boats" strategy is in place. There is no turning back. There are no escape options.

2. Enlist a mentor or coach.
   a. A coach or mentor provides a new perspective we cannot see ourselves.
   b. They help keep us accountable to our change.

3. Join a support group aligned around your change.
   a. A group consciousness reveals new perspectives and ideas.
   b. Your individual learning and growth accelerates within a group.
   c. Group learning holds you accountable.
   d. Group dynamics cause you to be accountable to yourself.

4. Create a supportive environment at work and home.
   a. We subconsciously couple with people and environments that we are exposed to daily.

b. Be purposeful in aligning your work and family environments to support your change.

5. Engage in the right community of people aligned with your change.

a. Find those communities with common values, ethics, and goals to support your change.

6. Support and contribute to others on the same journey.

a. A deep level of knowledge and engagement happens when you support and teach others.

b. Helping others to face their change supports you at staying in integrity with your own change.

I believe these 6 steps can help you stay on track with building and maintaining your Big, Bold, and Badass life.

GIVE YOURSELF A SHOT OF MOTIVATION—YOU ARE THE ONE AND ONLY!

You are incredibly unique! You and only you have come into this world to experience a path that is unique to you. No other human on this incredible planet of billions of people will share the same experience. Similar to your fingerprint, your powerful journey is full of one-of-a-kind experiences, insights, gifts, and talents that no one can mirror or match. When you think and feel this statement, it should bring a tingle to your spine, joy to your heart, and aliveness to your being. You are extremely significant and an essential part of this planet. You are an omnipotent force of creation!

Sometimes, we begin to question our power, and we allow external and internal noise to cloud our judgment of who we are, to the point of negating and diminishing our own life force and uniqueness. We do this by submitting to the pressure to be like everyone else. We try to conform and fit into the norm (whatever that is); but as this happens, our unique spirit begins to wane.

What do you do to keep your unique force and power alive and kicking at full strength? Motivation is one answer, and it is a tool that so many people hold with levity. I believe that motivation is a powerful tool to remind us of who we are and of how important our contribution is to the world. We are blessed to live in a time like no other, when we can get access to any and every type of motivational information with just a few taps on our smartphone! We can access the greatest motivational speakers and content any time of the day or night from any location. This is an amazing untapped gift right at our fingertips.

"People often say that motivation doesn't last.
Well, neither does bathing—that is why we recommend it daily."
– Zig Ziglar–

Motivation is important because it boosts your desire and keeps you moving without looking back. It is the confidence-enhancer or extra fuel that burns in you, preventing you from going back to your former state. There are many different types of motivational presentations and content on the Internet. You can find speeches, quotes, presentations, articles, books, radio programs, TV interviews, and movie clips. The options are endless.

My recommendation: Begin a new practice of using motivation as another tool in your tool belt to live a better life, to enhance your career, and to strengthen your relationships with others and with yourself. Search for that speech or speaker who has inspired you in the past, and start there. Explore by typing the word "motivation" into YouTube, search TED Talks, or just Google "motivation." This will help you to create a daily practice of motivation to open up the power of your unique and omnipotent self.

Find some subjects that work for you, and practice watching one video a day for a week, then see what happens.

Here are a few examples of motivational videos on YouTube. Go to the YouTube site, and type in these titles to view:

▸ "A Pep Talk from Kid President to You"

▸ "I'm the One"—Les Brown

▸ "Live your dreams"—Les Brown

▸ "Jessica's Daily Affirmations"

▸ "2014 Pep Talk"—Josh Shipp

Track your accomplishments and create a powerful interpretation for yourself. Part of coaching people is to help them see the progress they are making by revealing to them how they have changed. It is very difficult to feel change within ourselves. Since you are taking on the coaching role through this book, I recommend that you adopt the practice of tracking your success. Set up some metrics about where you are today, and then daily, weekly, monthly. Begin a simple journaling exercise to help keep you on track and aware of your progress. Success breeds success! Make it easy to win, and the wins will continue to come as you become your most powerful, engaged and confident Badass.

———————————

PROGRESS TOOLS

BADASS BLUEPRINT
AND
JOURNAL TEMPLATE

As mentioned previously, journaling your insights, values and "Ah-ha!" moments is a powerful tool to reference later for reinforcing the work you have done.

The forms in this section will help you keep record of your own personal Big, Bold and Bad fundamentals: **Foundation Building**, **Barrier Breaking**, and **Your Unique Purpose.**

BADASS BLUEPRINT

Keep track of the keywords you have gleaned from your exercises and applications for a quick reference at-a-glance of your Big, Bold, and Bad insights. This form is a reference sheet to remind you of the three building blocks of the blueprint:

- **Be Big defined:**
  Foundation Building—uncovering your foundation blocks. Identifying those unique talents, gifts and skills that make you a Badass.

- **Be Bold defined:**
  Courage & Barrier Breaking—stepping up to face and eliminate your barriers and building the courage to stand up for who you are in the world.

- **Be Bad defined:**
  Your Unique Purpose—mobilizing your Biggest & Boldest expression of yourself and pursuing your unique purpose to change the world.

JOURNAL TEMPLATES

The Journal templates will help guide you in organizing your journal notes from your exercises and applications. Write down your observations, insights, and keywords.

BADASS BLUEPRINT — KEYWORDS

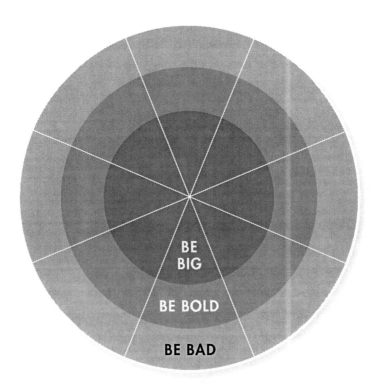

BE BIG (Foundation)_____

_____

_____

_____

BE BOLD (Courage & Barrier Breaking) _____

_____

_____

_____

BE BAD (Your Unique Purpose in the World)_____

_____

_____

_____

EXERCISE JOURNAL TEMPLATE

Keep a record of your exercise and application results
to solidify the lessons you're learning, and to make it
easier to refer back to as a refresher of your insights.

CHAPTER_____

EXERCISE: _____

Observation: _____

_____

_____

_____

_____

_____

_____

_____

Insight: _____

_____

_____

_____

_____

_____

_____

Keyword(s): _____

_____

_____

APPLICATION JOURNAL TEMPLATE

The following templates can help you format your journal. Write your keywords on your blueprint diagram as well to easily refer to your power words later on.

CHAPTER_____

APPLICATION: _____

Observation: _____

_____

_____

_____

_____

_____

_____

_____

_____

Insight: _____

_____

_____

_____

_____

_____

_____

_____

Keyword(s): _____

_____

_____

AFTERWORD

"If anything matters, everything matters."
—W. P. Young—

As I reflect on this quote from the book "The Shack" by William Paul Young, it is my hope that this is the conversation you are in. You matter, every bit of you matters. It is your obligation to you, your family, your community, your world and to your creator to allow ALL OF YOU to shine. My intention with this book is to be a voice in your life that reinforces, "You matter," beyond what you can imagine. Our life force is infinite beyond what we can feel, see or even understand. I hope through this book you have opened up your relationship with yourself, and are now aware of the gifts you have been given and the exceptional person you have become on this planet.

This book was designed to inspire you to STEP UP into your Bigness, your Boldness and your Badness- to be all that you can be, to awaken your Badass. With this perspective and power, you will be able to step forward into a new place, into a new life, into your unstoppable being and into all you can do.

Throughout my life's journey and especially in these last two years, I have come to realize that God is a very important part of my life. I have also come to realize that sharing my emotions and being forthright with who I am is really the most natural and best way to cope with the challenges I face. I am grateful that I was able to share my experience. The challenge I ask each and every one of you is to step up and allow yourself to feel again, to feel that greatness, that uninhibited power, that ultimate Badass that lives in each and every one of us. Allow it to shine in its biggest, boldest and baddest light.

Your unique BADASS is like a pebble in the pond of life. Your impact in this pond creates ripples which go out in endless rings throughout your life and to eternity. I wish you all the best of luck. God bless you on your powerful journey.

Steve Stefanik

BOOK STEVE STEFANIK TO SPEAK AT YOUR NEXT MEETING OR EVENT

"Steve is a high energy speaker. I asked him to speak to the top 10% of my sales organization. He brought a powerful message and unique delivery style which fully engaged and empowered my team of top producers. As a result, they all left ready to step up their game to the next level, full of actionable insights, new energy and confidence in who they are and what they do."

Jess Wible,
Vice president and managing officer

STEPPING UP YOUR GAME

Steve conducts his flagship presentations for corporate groups, small business owners and independent organizations who want to step up their game in business and life. Depending on your format, time availability, and meeting objectives, his presentations can run from 30 minutes to extensive multiple-day workshops. Steve promises to re-engage and empower your business, your people and your life.

For availability and booking information, call Steve at 408-355-3193 or email him at Steve@inhousecoach.com

WWW.INHOUSECOACH.COM

OFFERS, SERVICES AND COMMUNITY

▶ Share BE BAD! with your friends, family members, and colleagues.
Buy 50 copies and receive a 50% discount off the retail price.
Call 408-355-3193 for special pricing on larger quantities.

▶ Go to www.Be-Bad.com
Find more information about additional resources to support your new
Badass path. See our presentations, workshops, coaching offers, book
clubs, Badass community, videos and interviews.

▶ Follow our Facebook page to read Steve's addtional reflections.
Go to www.facebook.com/bebadbook.

▶ Check out our executive coaching site.
Go to www.inhousecoach.com.

▶ Send us your comments.
We'd like to hear your success stories, insights and any ideas you may
have for future reference and additional books.
Email to stefanikcoaching@yahoo.com.

CPSIA information can be obtained
at www.ICGtesting.com
Printed in the USA
FSOW02n1621170916
25037FS